Hands-On Guide to AgileOps

A Guide to Implementing Agile, DevOps, and SRE for Cloud Operations

Navin Sabharwal
Raminder Rathore
Udita Agrawal

Apress®

Hands-On Guide to AgileOps: A Guide to Implementing Agile, DevOps, and SRE for Cloud Operations

Navin Sabharwal
New Delhi, Delhi, India

Raminder Rathore
Ontario, Canada

Udita Agrawal
Ghaziabad, India

ISBN-13 (pbk): 978-1-4842-7504-7
https://doi.org/10.1007/978-1-4842-7505-4

ISBN-13 (electronic): 978-1-4842-7505-4

Managing Director, Apress Media LLC: Welmoed Spahr
Acquisitions Editor: Aditee Mirashi
Development Editor: James Markham
Coordinating Editor: Mark Powers
Copyeditor: Kimberly Wimpsett

Cover designed by eStudioCalamar

Cover image by Pixabay (www.pixabay.com)

Distributed to the book trade worldwide by Springer Science+Business Media New York, 1 New York Plaza, Suite 4600, New York, NY 10004-1562, USA. Phone 1-800-SPRINGER, fax (201) 348-4505, e-mail orders-ny@ springer-sbm.com, or visit www.springeronline.com. Apress Media, LLC is a California LLC and the sole member (owner) is Springer Science + Business Media Finance Inc (SSBM Finance Inc). SSBM Finance Inc is a **Delaware** corporation.

For information on translations, please e-mail booktranslations@springernature.com; for reprint, paperback, or audio rights, please e-mail bookpermissions@springernature.com.

Apress titles may be purchased in bulk for academic, corporate, or promotional use. eBook versions and licenses are also available for most titles. For more information, reference our Print and eBook Bulk Sales web page at http://www.apress.com/bulk-sales.

Any source code or other supplementary material referenced by the author in this book is available to readers on GitHub via the book's product page, located at www.apress.com/9781484275047. For more detailed information, please visit http://www.apress.com/source-code.

Printed on acid-free paper

Table of Contents

About the Authors

Navin Sabharwal has more than 23 years of industry experience. He is a thought leader and head of strategy and development in the areas of agile, cloud computing, DevSecOps, AIOps, FinOps, artificial intelligence, and SaaS product engineering. He holds seven patents in the areas of AI and machine learning. He has authored 15+ books on cloud capacity management, observability, DevOps, cloud automation, containerization, Google AutoML, BERT, and NLP. He can be reached at Navinsabharwal@gmail.com and www.linkedin.com/in/navinsabharwal.

Raminder Rathore is a DevOps practitioner with two decades of IT experience. Currently working as the practice head at HCL Technologies, she helps customers drive transformative programs on agility and resiliency. She has been successful in enabling and completing enterprise-wide programs on DevOps and agile, including defining organization roadmaps on transformation, process optimization, and automation tools rationalization (including open source and COTS); planning and architecting CI/CD pipelines; service catalog designing for cloud platforms; building accelerators for end-to-end product traceability; and coaching teams on adopting agile ways of working. She can be reached at raminder.rathore@gmail.com and https://www.linkedin.com/in/raminder-devops-practitioner/.

Udita Agrawal is a DevOps practitioner with more than 17 years of IT experience. She has diverse experience in agile and DevOps implementation in development, testing, data analytics, and infrastructure operations. Currently working as a senior DevOps consultant at HCL Technologies, she has been working with different customers in enabling and improving practices and processes in agile and DevOps. She also has an interest in delivering training to teams in the same area. She can be reached at `udita.agrawal@gmail.com` and `www.linkedin.com/in/udita-agrawal-DevOps-Consultant`.

About the Technical Reviewer

Afzaal Ahmad Zeeshan is a developer advocate at Adyen and likes .NET Core and Node.js for regular, everyday development. He is an expert in cloud, mobile, and API development. Afzaal has experience with the Azure platform and enjoys building cross-platform libraries/software with .NET Core. He has written *DevSecOps for .NET Core* for Apress, as well as many online technical articles.

Afzaal is an Alibaba Cloud MVP; twice he has been awarded Microsoft MVP status for his thought leadership in software development, five times CodeProject MVP status for technical writing and mentoring, and four times C# Corner MVP status in the same field. Afzaal is an active open source contributor on GitHub and GitLab. You can find him as `afzaal-ahmad-zeeshan` and `@afzaalvirgoboy`.

Acknowledgments

To my family, Shweta and Soumil, for always being there by my side and sacrificing their time for my intellectual and spiritual pursuits. This and other accomplishments of my life wouldn't have been possible without your love and support.

To my mom and my sister: for their love and support as always; without your blessings, nothing is possible.

To my co-authors, Raminder and Udita: thank you for the hard work and quick turnarounds to deliver this book. It was an enriching experience, and I am looking forward to working with you again soon.

To my team at HCL, who have been a source of inspiration with their hard work, ever-engaging technical conversations, and technical depth: Raminder, Udita, Piyush, Amit, Sarvesh, Subramani, Praveen, Sagar, Amit Dwivedi, Sandeep, Shakuntala, Vasand, Punith, Nitin, Vivek, Gaurav Bali, Arvind Gautam, and Inderpal.

Thank you to Celestine, Aditee, and the entire team at Apress for turning our ideas into reality. It has been an amazing experience authoring with you, and over the years, the speed of decision-making and the editorial support have been excellent.

Thank you, goddess Saraswati, for guiding us to the path of knowledge and spirituality.

असतो मा साद गमय, तमसो मा ज्योतिर् गमय, मृत्योर मा अमृतम् गमय

(Asato Ma Sad Gamaya, Tamaso Ma Jyotir Gamaya, Mrityor Ma Amritam Gamaya)

Lead us from ignorance to truth, lead us from darkness to light, lead us from death to immortality.

Preface

Agile has transformed the way software development is done today. Digital organizations and startups have embraced and reaped the benefits of agile and DevOps. However, the infrastructure and cloud operations world has largely remained untouched by the agile movement. The infrastructure and operations world has largely continued using IT service management and ITIL for running scale operations.

There are many best practices that can be adopted for operations, namely, agile, DevOps, site reliability engineering (SRE), lean, ITIL, IT4IT; however, there is no guidance available on how to use these processes in the IT infrastructure world. Similarly, there are tools available for running these processes, but there is no guidance available on how to use these tools for running operations.

With the advent of cloud computing, it has become equally important to understand the benefits of IaaS, PaaS, or SaaS for enterprises. There has been a shift from a monolithic to microservices architecture to improve the availability and up time for environments and applications.

There are numerous agile methods like Scrum, Kanban, and scrumban and different scaled agile frameworks such as SAFe®, Spotify, LeSS, and Nexus, DAD. Enterprises find it difficult to decide which agile framework and method to adopt. They can be easily adopted for operations both for on-premise and the cloud.

This book is a hands-on guide on how to adopt agile, DevOps, and SRE practices; how to build a roadmap for them; and how to select the most suitable processes for your organization to achieve higher reliability, agility, and lower costs while running cloud and infrastructure operations.

Specifically, the book covers the following in detail:

- Agile in software development versus operations
- ITIL, IT4IT, and lean, and their relevance in agile operations
- Scrum, Kanban, and scrumban agile methods
- Scaled agile frameworks for agile operations
- Site reliability engineering and integration with agile and DevOps

- DevOps and applicability in agile operations

- Infrastructure as a code and its integration with pipelines

- Agile stories and examples for operations

- Creating a team structure for agile operations

- Creating a roadmap for the adoption of agile in operations

- Case study for agile operations

We welcome you to this exciting journey of discovering new ways of running IT operations by leveraging various processes, methods, and techniques to create an efficient, cost-effective, and agile model that serves the needs of modern digital enterprises.

We will also be creating content and best practices on a continuous basis that you can view on the companion site at `www.AgileInfraOps.com`.

CHAPTER 1

Introduction

In this chapter, we will be introducing agile and its relevance in bridging the gap between the development and operations teams that traditionally work in silos. The topics that will be covered in this chapter are as follows:

- Agile history

- Evolving software teams

- Bridging the gap between Dev and Ops

- Complementing agile with DevOps

- Agility in infrastructure operations

- Agile Manifesto

In the 21st century, digital enterprises are constantly innovating and experiencing advancements across all fields such as science and technology, economics, urbanization, biotechnology and medicine, and many other areas. Each of these sectors is evolving based on customer needs and becomes successful when it quickly adapts to changing demands. Businesss in these sectors also understand the importance of data and leveraging technology to instantly access this data. Quick access to data helps organizations make wise decisions, prepare organization roadmaps, budget for new and innovative programs, and get prepared for the future. All this has been made possible by the adoption of technology platforms that enable companies to access reusable components, revive quickly from failures, and stay globally connected. The management and maintenance of the technology platforms are taken care of by the information technology (IT) department, the backbone serving internal and external customers for their various IT needs. These IT teams have also evolved with time and become agile to support the digital businesses. Teams are willing to transform quickly so that they offer timely services to their customers. Agility for them is no longer optional; instead, it has become a necessity. Organizations today leverage IT teams not only for addressing their

© Navin Sabharwal, Raminder Rathore, and Udita Agrawal 2022
N. Sabharwal et al., *Hands-On Guide to AgileOps*, https://doi.org/10.1007/978-1-4842-7505-4_1

basic operational tasks but also for building new systems rapidly that are compliant and secure. Typical waterfall application development projects took months or even years; with agile methodologies, new updates are rolled out weekly or monthly. There are organizations that are rolling out updates daily or even multiple times a day. As technology and processes evolve, IT teams are scaling with new agile ways of working.

There are numerous success stories on how agile adoption has helped organizations to quickly scale, fail fast, deliver in iterations, and excel by prioritizing their requirements based on customer feedback. The Agile Manifesto with its 12 principles is the key driver that is making organizations successful. In fact, many organizations have identified and designed custom agile methods that best suit their ecosystem of people, process, and technology. Since inception to its current state, agile has transformed the way products and solutions are delivered to consumers. The concept is not restricted to the IT world but has benefitted many non-IT companies too.

Though the concept of agile in the IT industry has been around for more than two decades, this will remain an evolving subject for many more years to come. Every company that is planning to adopt agile or has adopted agile has a clear vision, which is to "deliver fast" with no compromises on security and quality. To address the growing market needs and frequently changing customer demands, the ability to deploy quickly is possible through highly effective autonomous teams practicing agile principles. Over the years, various methods and tools have been designed to simplify the adoption of agile across multiple industries. New operating frameworks have been introduced that comprise optimized processes and new roles and responsibilities that nurture the culture of collaboration and accountability. A team's location is now no more a constraint. Companies that have a cloud and digitalization roadmap are rapidly moving into agile. Agile models like Nexus, Spotify, etc., are being adopted at scale. Alongside the agile movement, new roles like site reliability engineer are emerging. These new roles are growing in demand in most organizations, and the expectation is to reduce dependency on human actions and introduce automation as much as possible. Organizations are cross-skilling and reskilling their teams to work in agile development and operations.

Some organizations start with a bottom-up approach wherein they first target "being agile," which means they start with smaller application teams or infrastructure operations teams and onboard them to agile ways of working. Then they slowly transition toward enterprise adoption by "doing agile," which means there is visibility and accountability at all levels. Various agile tools and techniques are leveraged to ensure the organizational transformation is successful and teams practice the culture of trust and transparency. There are best practices, publications, and guidance available aplenty on agile and its adoption in the application development space; however, when it comes to adopting agile in the operations area, it is still dominated by ITSM methodologies like ITIL. This book will share experiences and best practices for adopting agile in the infrastructure, cloud, and application operation spaces. It also looks at the needs and the reasons for being agile in the infrastructure world, which focuses on agility, improved visibility and communication, team accountability, continuous learning, increased productivity, and customer experience. Though agile has been used extensively across organizations in the software development space, its adoption and usage in the infrastructure space is still a gray area. The practices of Scrum, Kanban, XP, etc., are well documented, and guidance around these are available in abundance; however, when it comes to "what" and "how" to adopt these methodologies in the infrastructure operations space, there are missing links. There are multiple best practices, methodologies, and working models available on site reliability engineering (SRE), DevOps, and infrastructure as code (IaC), which have overlapping guidance, processes, and roles. This book connects all these concepts and provides rich guidance to run end-to-end development and operations successfully. It also compares the frameworks and runs through different scenarios, allowing teams to choose the best method and operating model for their organizations.

There is a lot of existing literature and guidance available on adopting agile in the software development space. This publication aims to bring these to the infrastructure and cloud operations world and addresses the following:

- Evolution of traditional to modern agile ways of working

- Need for being agile in infrastructure and cloud operations

- Emerging roles in the agile world

- Understanding different agile methods and how to implement them

- Comparing various agile methods and benefits

- New technology platforms for adopting agile

Agile History: The Starting Point

Officially, agile's inception started during early 1990s when there were a few organizations that practiced extreme programming (XP), the Scrum methodology, and other agile processes to speed up their delivery timelines. In early 2000s, the agile principles were formalized into a manifesto and published for wider consumption. But its actual acceptance in IT happened in early 2010s. Agile was always well accepted and preached by development teams, and it became a de facto standard for delivering software. The four core guiding principles of agile embraced the new culture that responded to instant changes and focused on team collaboration. Other departments like infrastructure operations still continued with their traditional approach, detailed documentation, multiple approval gates, and manual lengthy processes. There existed two worlds in the product development space; one was agile driven, and the other was nonagile and followed rigid processes and approval workflows and the waterfall model for planning and delivering.

Interestingly, it was not just IT that benefitted from the concepts of agile; there were other domains that leveraged agile tools and practices like defense, aerospace, etc. There is an interesting story of a logistics officer in the Royal Navy named Paul Jackson who believed in agile principles and benefitted from them in his very first assignment on a new ship. On this first assignment, he studied that the maintenance program for the ship could be shortened from weeks to just five days using agile principles. In these five days, he had to ensure that the ship's staff had enough supplies while on their journey for 90 days in the sea. He started running daily standups every day to prioritize and align with the needs instead of executing on a detailed plan. Each day's meeting helped him and his team to reprioritize as needed. Finally, the efforts spent in iterations on these five days helped Paul finish his job successfully. The iterative approach helped Paul and his team, and they became agile believers. There are hundreds of success stories across the globe that signify that short iterative cycles with an agile mindset help teams accomplish their targets easily. The idea behind agile's success was iterative delivery, which was better than the traditional waterfall approach of delivering products and services in a sequential manner with integration testing coming in at the very end of the process. The adoption was not just about new processes and ways of working, but it also introduced new role definitions. Roles like Scrum master, product manager, etc., were introduced that motivated professionals to upscale, and teams underwent structural changes to address the new model of delivery. The expectation was clear that teams should deliver in small iterations that were named *sprints*, and these deliverables were called a *minimum viable product* (MVP). An MVP can be visualized as a prototype with enough features that can be verified by customers. Feedback from customers on MVPs served as enhancements for future product development and changes. At the end of each sprint, the focus was to get feedback from the customers or stakeholders and implement these iteratively so that each product developed met customer expectations. This method helped teams to happily accept changes as they moved ahead in their delivery cycle. This was easy for a development team, but applying these principles in the infrastructure world is still a challenge. See Figure 1-1.

DID YOU KNOW?

THERE IS SOMETHING CALLED EVP TOO!

While an MVP – Minimal Viable Product is released to the public, on the other hand an EVP is an Exceptional Viable Product that is only released to selected customers/groups.

Figure 1-1. *Did you know?*

Evolving Software Teams: Drifting to New Ways of Working

Let's take a step back and look at the different teams that are part of a product lifecycle. A traditional software team comprises five major groups: development, testing/QA, security, operations, and governance/PMO. Though each team is committed to delivering fast, they practice their own set of rules, and this leads to delays or issues. Communication across different groups is also a challenge. As time progressed and the agile principles started getting popular and having a positive impact on software delivery, development groups adopted the agile principles quickly. But other teams lagged behind due to their traditional methods such as manual checkpoints, multiple approval gates for compliance and security checks, relaxed SLAs, etc.

The infrastructure operations continued their rigid ways of working. This was not without reason, and there were technical and process limitations that mandated the way infrastructure teams operated. A key reason for the rigidness was their accountability that ensured that the systems were reliable, were highly available, complied with architectural standards, were secure and verified, and were approved by designated approval authorities. Also, the on-premise infrastructure had to be run in a planned waterfall model, and detailed planning was needed to ensure every individual component worked with the other hardware components. Since the infrastructure teams dealt with hardware rather than software, it was required to have detailed planning, architecture, and documentation. Any miss in the hardware components would set back the project by months since new components had to be procured, shipped, and then installed. Some of the processes are also essential for reliable and secure software development. To ensure reliability and security, elaborate change and release management processes with multiple steps and multiple stakeholder approvers were put in place. These processes became part of the daily routine and culture, and after a while they became so entrenched in the minds of people that any deviation from these processes became an organizational change management problem. Thus, on one hand, the development teams were delivering periodically and wanted to deploy new changes instantly. On the other hand, infrastructure operations had defined schedules, and making frequent changes to the system was a Herculean task for them. The infrastructure operations team is the backbone for any organization since it manages the servers and platforms, integrates with security, and works with other teams to ensure that the systems are compliant to the defined policies, procedures, and statutory requirements.

This gap between development and infrastructure operations teams existed for many years. But with evolving changes in IT and the availability of new platforms, organizations understood that they needed to change their ways of working. They needed to bring the infrastructure operations team closer to the development teams and enable themselves on agile and continuous delivery, which is the only way to enable software to be rolled out to the customer faster. Otherwise, it would be coded, tested, and integrated but not deployed on production systems and hence unavailable to the customers, thus defeating the whole purpose of an agile and iterative delivery. All this was made possible because of a technology shift to the cloud where infrastructure could be created and destroyed using code just like software components. This tectonic technology shift now impacts the way teams are structured, skilled, and operate. See Figure 1-2.

DID YOU KNOW?

NUMBER OF PROGRAMMING LANGUAGES THAT EXIST?

There are about 700 programming languages that exist today (according to Wikipedia).
Also 1 in 3 developers are now writing code before even finishing high school.

Figure 1-2. *Did you know?*

Bridging the Dev and Ops Gap

So, while at one end, the development teams were always looking out to push new code in production, the operations teams resisted changes. A common scenario that has been evident is where the development teams are in need of an environment, but they have to follow a tedious process to request this new infrastructure that includes multiple approvals. This traditional process had a long turnaround time that results in frustration for the development teams. There are many organizations where such requests were delivered by their operations team in weeks rather than days. While development teams wants to be quick, operations slow down their speed. See Figure 1-3.

Development	Operation
• **Driven by** Change	• **Driven by** Stability
• **Deliver Project on** Time & Budget	• **Zero** Downtime
• **Demands** Frequent Releases	• **Encourage** Fewer Releases
• **Demand of** Consistent Platforms	• **Scalable** Platform

Figure 1-3. *The Dev and Ops wishlist*

With changes in the business environment and availability of latest technologies, organizations have accepted the fact that agility and DevOps are the need of the hour and that they need to quickly identify ways to bridge the rift between the development and operations teams. So, it is not just agile that is to be nurtured, but there is a need to embrace DevOps across all teams in the organization. Most organizations are looking for quick deployments and ways to empower their teams so that they can have access to instant infrastructure and an end-to-end visibility of their product lifecycle. All this is becoming possible through people motivation, upskilling, investments in new technology, and streamlined processes to reduce turnaround time.

DevOps: Complementing Agile

The term DevOps was coined by Patrick Debois, a Belgian IT consultant and agile practitioner in 2009. The core principles of DevOps are providing better integration between developments and operations, reducing the friction between the development and operations teams, and ensuring realization of the agile promise of faster product delivery to customers. DevOps covers the entire product lifecycle from design to operations and aims to achieve continuous deployment.

DevOps promotes the following key principles:

- *No more silos*: Greater collaboration across the entire product lifecycle and between development and operations teams will result in higher productivity and fewer operations issues.

- *Failures are normal*: Preventing all failures is impossible, but DevOps focuses on learning from failures and treating them as opportunities to improve.

- *Gradual changes*: Incremental and gradual changes to the environment in smaller sprints are aimed at increasing throughput, getting working software in the hands of the consumer, and realizing the aim of agile by moving to a model of continuous deployment.

- *Automation*: Automation is the key focus of DevOps; it aims to achieve continuous integration, testing, development, and deployment and to eliminate manual steps.

- *Metrics*: Changes should be measured, and the impact of changes should be analyzed to drive continual service improvement.

Agility in Infrastructure Operations: Need of the Hour

While automation is low-hanging fruit that can be achieved, the most challenging part is bringing the development and operations teams together and cultivating an environment of trust and accountability. While development teams practice agile, the infrastructure operations team needs to get up to speed. They need to be mentored on the need to do operations in an agile way and also upscale themselves on automated platforms that can ease their job and reduce toil. In the past decade, the rise of infrastructure as code has gained momentum and is resulting in a higher level of abstraction and automation at the infrastructure layer. Additionally, there has been an increase in the adoption of cloud platforms that is accelerating the process of bridging the gap between the development and infrastructure operations teams as well as providing the right foundation for automation and infrastructure as code. Development teams are becoming empowered since they get access to spin up and decommission dev and test environments as needed, and on the other hand, the infrastructure operations teams have the tools and technologies to enable faster deployments that are now made possible through automated pipelines. Teams at both ends have realized the benefits and the need to be agile.

In fact, this served as an example for many organizations that responded to sudden changes in the environment and were quickly able to release new functionality and features thereby increasing adoption of their technologies and their customer base and revenue.

The Agile Manifesto: Simple Guiding Principles

The Agile Manifesto was written in February 2001 by a group of software and methodology experts. The manifesto is simple to understand. It states the agile values mentioned in Figure 1-4. It emphasizes that the values mentioned on both the sides of Figure 1-4 will exist; however, more focus and effort should be put on the values mentioned on the left side. Like individuals and interactions, processes and tools both will exist, but more focus should be given to establish interactions with individuals than processes and tools.

Figure 1-4. *Agile values*

While agile serves the purpose of delivering fast, it needs to be complemented with a true DevOps culture that connects teams and processes through automation. The essence is not to just streamline the processes but also focus on people and tools. While agile focuses on the development teams, DevOps, on the other hand, promises to bind teams together (Dev, QA, Ops). Both agile and DevOps act as an excellent mediator for implementing the principles of coupling and cohesiveness; hence, DevOps and agile complement each other. While agile refers to an iterative approach of delivering software, DevOps refers to the ways of working between development and operations (an end-to-end engineering practice). It is an interesting journey to note how organizations are adopting both agile and DevOps and responding to the changing ecosystem.

This book encapsulates all the previous topics and synergizes them with the new trends that are emerging in the agile and DevOps world, especially for infrastructure and cloud operations teams. Several new methods, roles, and expectations have evolved, and we will walk through them with real-life examples. The idea is to provide a 360-degree view on how product teams can function effectively using the right agile methods and tools. We will look at real-life examples of implementing agile methods like Kanban and Scrum with tools like Jira, Jenkins, etc. There are various examples cited throughout the book that include infrastructure and cloud operations story writing, story estimation techniques, and how cloud technologies and platforms are helping teams build and deliver services quickly. The technique of failing fast is essential, and this is resonated in this book with various methods that help teams to fail and recover. We will focus on best practices that infrastructure and cloud operations should leverage to be successful in the agile and DevOps worlds.

Summary

Agile is an important need today. Besides software application development teams, even infrastructure operations teams are adopting an agile mindset to deliver quickly. These teams practice agile principles that focus on delivering value in small increments, continuously monitoring feedback and fostering effective collaboration. The introduction to new platforms like cloud, container technology, automated deployments, etc., are accelerating the path to newer ways of working that are no longer an option but a need. New roles are also evolving that are making teams more accountable and connected. This book is a starter kit for all the teams, especially the cloud and infrastructure operations teams, that are looking for guidance and recommendations toward adopting agile and DevOps.

CHAPTER 2

Traditional Infrastructure Operations

In this chapter, we will discuss the traditional way of working in infrastructure operations where IT service management processes are used and agile has not been adopted for operations. A majority of organizations are running infrastructure and cloud operations in this model today, while a few organizations have successfully migrated to agile ways of operations. The topics that will be covered in this chapter are as follows:

- IT service management approach

- Drawbacks of traditional InfraOps teams

- Need for change

An infrastructure operations team is an IT team that specializes in managing the environments (on-premises, cloud, etc.) and may be providing services to both internal and external customers. An internal customer could be the development teams that request services around provisioning, upgrading, and managing the environments (such as dev, test, production, etc.). External customers are users who access production system that host applications. An environment can be visualized as an integrated set of components such as compute, storage, networks, backups, security, monitoring, management, and everything needed for running that machine in a compliant and secure manner. The InfraOps team is responsible for monitoring, managing, maintaining, upgrading, installing, and configuring the components, as well as maintaining security. The team works closely with governance and security teams for regular validations of the systems in use. Anything that has to be introduced in the system is well tested and approved through a well-defined set of processes. These teams adopt and run operations using best practices and processes aligned to ITIL, IT4IT, etc., that track and audit their actions. For many years these teams have operated in silos and followed their own processes and principles, and they have limited collaboration with the application development teams. See Figure 2-1.

© Navin Sabharwal, Raminder Rathore, and Udita Agrawal 2022
N. Sabharwal et al., *Hands-On Guide to AgileOps*, https://doi.org/10.1007/978-1-4842-7505-4_2

DID YOU KNOW?

What is an I&O Organization?

An I&O Organization is an Infrastructure and Operations team that follow a typical hierarchy structure that is responsible for services like compute, storage, backup, network, database, etc.

Figure 2-1. *Did you know?*

ITSM Approach

The infrastructure operations team acts as a backbone service. The team services multiple internal teams with various infrastructure needs but typically operates on rigid processes. Interestingly, the team has been successful for a long time, thanks to frameworks like ITIL (formerly an acronym for Information Technology Infrastructure Library) that helped teams to follow defined processes. The teams have a well-defined support curriculum that includes OS and kernel support, physical server and VM maintenance, server provisioning, server patching, backups, storage, databases, user identity management, active directory, high availability/disaster recovery (HA/DR), server monitoring, etc. The focus is on ensuring that the systems are secure and are compliant, that each step of the process is defined, and that every action is logged and measured through service level objectives and service level agreements. The process of deploying new changes in production is well planned and is executed after multiple approvals from the respective technical lines of businesses. These deployments are planned during off-hours or during weekends. There are also processes and procedures for backing up and restoring and in the case of a change failure reverting to the original configuration. Multiple teams from infrastructure, virtualization, storage, network, disaster recovery, business continuity plan (BCP), change managers, and application teams are required during large and complex datacenter changes. Requests for provisioning new infrastructure also follow a stringent process.

Dev and QA teams have struggled with this traditional approach since their target to deliver quickly is compromised due to a lack of agility in the infrastructure space. Developers and testers have to wait for environments to be provisioned, and this delays their milestones. See Figure 2-2.

Figure 2-2. *Reality check for traditional ops*

Most InfraOps teams operate 24/7, and application development teams reach out to them through information technology service management (ITSM) tools like ServiceNow, Remedy, Jira, etc. The InfraOps teams provide support across different areas with strict SLAs. Let's now deep dive into ITIL, which has been the backbone of IT service management processes.

ITIL comprises detailed practices and processes for implementing IT service management. It can be visualized as a catalog that lists processes, tasks, and checklists required to accomplish services. In other words, it is a collection of best practices that are needed to manage and improve IT services and support. The service lifecycle focuses on coordination across various departments, teams, and processes that are necessary for managing the lifecycle of IT services. An IT service is provided to customers by an IT service provider that focuses on a customer's business processes and needs. The ITIL 4.0 generic processes are laid out by ITIL at `https://www.axelos.com/best-practice-solutions/itil`.

ITSM has four key pillars, called the *four Ps*, as shown in Figure 2-3.

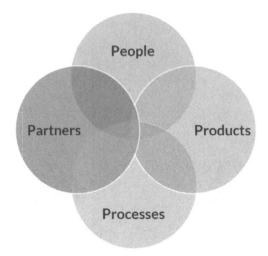

Figure 2-3. *ITSM's four Ps*

Processes: Processes should be measurable and have specific results that are quantifiable, that are customer centric, and that deliver value to them meeting their expectations.

People: People are all the required stakeholders who are either creating a service or consuming a service within an organization.

Products: Products refer to the tools that are used by the IT service staff to implement the ITIL processes. Tools that are required are integrated and used to execute the organizational processes.

Partners: Organizations have many partners who work along with them on IT services. This requires support agreements and requirements to be communicated to the partners.

There are various roles in ITSM, listed here:

- *Process owner*: The process owner owns the process, is involved in the process design, designs the strategy, and also defines process key performance indicators (KPIs).

- *Process manager*: The process manager manages the resources, aligns resources on different roles, tracks process performance, and provides improvements in the process.

- *Process practitioner*: The process practitioner works on multiple tasks of a process and ensures accuracy. This person also updates the status of the tasks in respective tools for a smooth handover.

- *Service owner*: The service owner is accountable for the service delivery and is the primary customer contact. The service owner also plays the role of business analyst or service requirement and identifies improvements in services.

The framework comprises five essential stages.

Service Strategy

Service Strategy focuses on the service lifecycle and describes how to design, develop, and implement service management (see Figure 2-4). It defines the target customers and what value the service will deliver. It helps service providers to meet business objectives. This stage involves key processes such as the following:

- *Demand Management*: This relates to understanding the customer requirements. It is necessary to meet customer expectations by providing services along with agreed warranty terms.

- *Financial Management*: This facilitates budgeting and cost of services and performs financial reviews.

- *Service Portfolio Management*: Service Portfolio is set of services managed by a service provider. These services are part of the service catalog. It has services that are active and can be consumed by consumers.

- *Business Relationship Management*: This is all about customer interaction and communication. The customer interacts with business relationship managers for projects. They manage the business relationship with stakeholders.

Figure 2-4. *Service Strategy*

Service Design

Service Design includes designing services based on the business requirements and objectives that provide value to the customer (see Figure 2-5). It focuses on delivering effective IT solutions that are aligned to business needs. It describes the "how" part of designing services and processes. It includes key processes such as the following:

- *Service Level Management*: This ensures that specific and measurable targets are developed for all IT services. It is directly related to customer satisfaction as it relates to how quickly issues are responded to, as well as their resolution and quality. It includes service level requirements, service level agreements, operational level agreements, underpinning contracts, and service improvement plans.

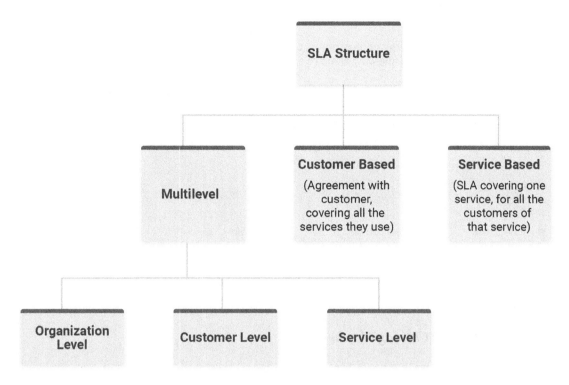

Figure 2-5. *Service level management*

- *Supplier Management*: This stage manages suppliers and the services they supply to customers.

- *Service Catalog Management*: This contains all the operational and planned services and their details including status, interfaces, and dependencies. The details in service catalog should be updated regularly including with automatic live updates. Figure 2-6 shows a sample catalog and its creation.

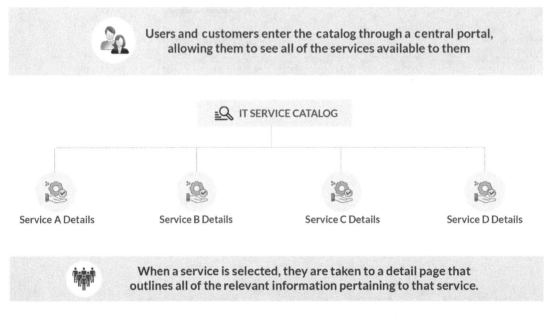

Figure 2-6. *Service Catalog Management*

- *Availability Management*: In the current era, it is important that the IT infrastructure and applications are both always available. This stage designs, implements, measures, manages, and improves the IT service and component availability. Availability is expressed as a percentage, as shown here:

Availability = (Agreed Service Time – Downtime) * 100

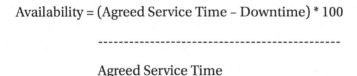

Agreed Service Time

- *Capacity Management*: The goal here is to provide the required infrastructure in a cost-effective manner and ensure its effective utilization. Organizations are transitioning from on-premise infrastructure to the cloud to have better infrastructure utilization. Capacity Management changes drastically when organizations move from on-premise infrastructure to on-demand infrastructure. FinOps plays a key role in cloud capacity management and needs to be incorporated as a function to manage the cloud resources and their consumption along with the financial management of the various models of consumption available in cloud computing environments.

- *Service Continuity Management*: This ensures the required services can be resumed in the case of a failure or disaster. It includes tasks to perform risk assessment and risk management to proactively avoid the risks or disasters from occurring (see Figure 2-7). It aims at reducing risks by developing a recovery plan to restore business activities if they are interrupted.

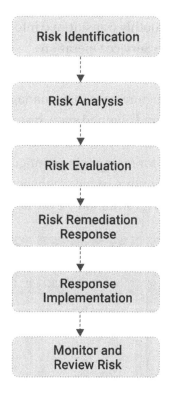

Figure 2-7. *A risk framework*

- *Information Security Management*: This aligns IT security with business compliance. It enforces security in all aspects in all services and service management activities. It also deals with risk analysis and risk management.

- *Design Coordination*: This is a single point of coordination among all activities and processes. It also ensures the objectives of the Service Design stage are fulfilled and handed over to the Service Transition stage.

Service Transition

Service Transition explains how to manage the transition of a new or modified service (see Figure 2-8). It comprises key processes such as the following

- *Transition Planning and Support*: This involves planning and coordination for the services across all relevant stakeholders like suppliers, service teams, etc. It also ensures the requirements from Service Strategy are smoothly transitioned into developed services from the design stage to Service Operation.

- *Service Asset and Configuration Management*: All the components of services and infrastructure have to be managed. Its configuration details such as current and planned state, historical information, etc., need to be maintained. The configuration management database (CMDB) is widely used for maintaining configuration details for infrastructure. It also supports service management processes by providing configuration information for the assets.

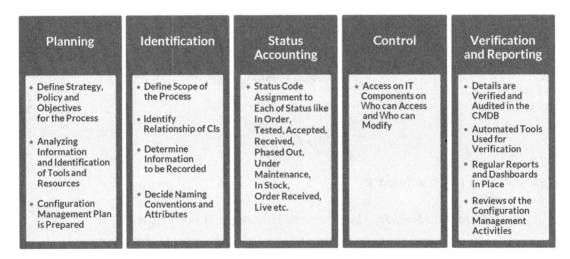

Figure 2-8. *Service Transition*

- *Change Management*: The objective of the Change Management process is to ensure that changes are recorded or entered in the respective ALM (Application Lifecycle Management) tool and then evaluated; discussed in the change review board or meeting; and then prioritized, planned, and implemented on the planned date and time (see Figure 2-9). Change Management needs standardized methods and procedures to be used for handling the changes effectively and efficiently. All the changes to services and configuration items are updated in the configuration management system.

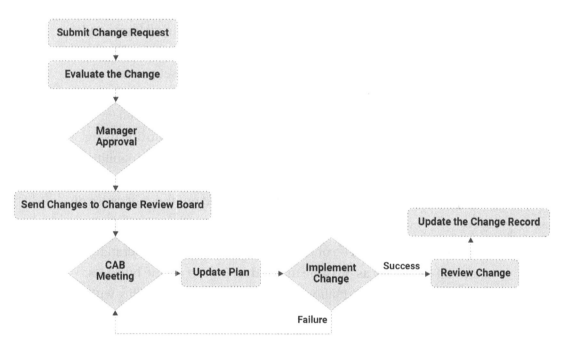

Figure 2-9. *Change Management process*

- *Release and Deployment Management*: The objective is to build, install, test, and deploy applications or services in the target environments. This process ensures that the new or updated service or configurations are delivering the correct requirements. There are various automated tools that can be used to automate the Release and Deployment Management activities.

- *Knowledge Management*: The objective is to harness and harvest knowledge for reuse rather that re-inventing and re-discovering knowledge. This is beneficial when the service knowledge management system is created, maintained, and regularly updated.

Service Operation

Service Operation is about coordinating and performing activities that are required for the smooth running of services (see Figure 2-10). It ensures that the required services are delivered as per the agreed upon service levels. It includes key processes such as the following:

- *Event Management*: The objective is to detect events at all levels and take appropriate actions to handle the events. The automated tools monitor the events and generate alerts based on the set process for them. It provides a basis for proactive monitoring and service improvement. This has now evolved into a new domain called Observability, and the emphasis is on end-to-end monitoring using logs, metrics, events, and traces. This includes advanced capabilities to provide an end-to-end view and provide correlation across infrastructure and applications to be able to find out the root cause of issues.

- *Incident Management*: The objective is to restore service operations to normal as quickly as possible to avoid an impact on the business. It focuses on delivering quality services and higher availability with minimal downtime. The incidents can be failures that are detected by Event Management or reported by users.

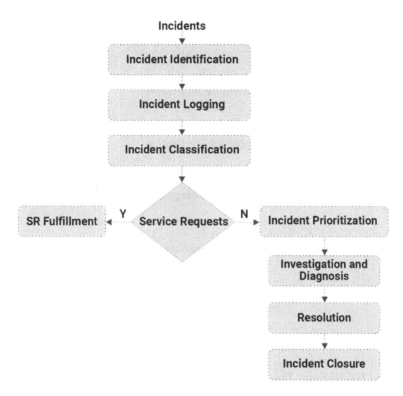

Figure 2-10. *Incident Management process*

- *Problem Management*: The objective is to prevent incidents by finding their root cause of occurrence (see Figure 2-11). Eliminate the incidents that occur periodically and focus on minimizing the impact for incidents that cannot be prevented.

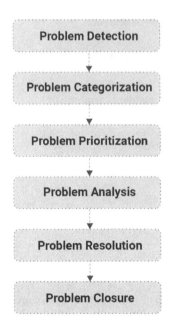

Figure 2-11. *Problem Management lifecycle*

- *Request Fulfillment*: The objective is to fulfill the service requests raised by users. Service requests fall into different categories such as informational ones on status of a service, access requests, complaints, etc.

- *Access Management*: The objective is to provide authorized users with the required access rights to use a service. Access Management follows the policies that are listed for Security and Availability Management.

Continual Service Improvement

This stage focuses on how to re-align IT services to match business changes. It matures the IT services by implementing identified improvement areas. It follows the famous Deming cycle, which has four stages: Plan, Do, Check, and Act. It also follows the seven steps in the Service Improvement process (see Figure 2-12). See Figure 2-13 for a tip.

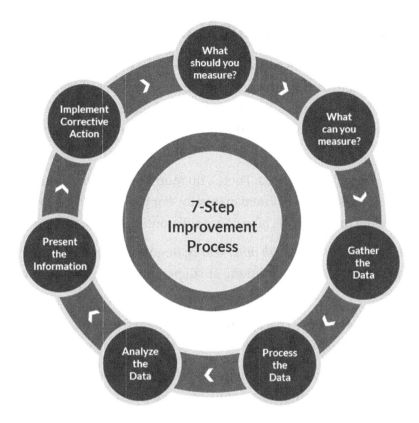

Figure 2-12. *Seven-step improvement process*

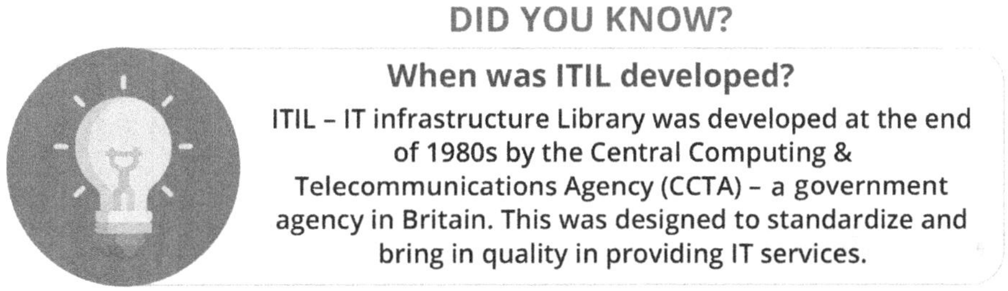

DID YOU KNOW?

When was ITIL developed?

ITIL – IT infrastructure Library was developed at the end of 1980s by the Central Computing & Telecommunications Agency (CCTA) – a government agency in Britain. This was designed to standardize and bring in quality in providing IT services.

Figure 2-13. *Did you know?*

Drawbacks with Traditional InfraOps Teams

The InfraOps team can continue with the way it has been operating all these years, but times have changed, and there is an urge to move to a new operating model that is more aligned with newer technologies such as cloud, containerization, and infrastructure as code. Let's take a look at some of the drawbacks of the traditional infrastructure operations model:

- *Structured but rigid process*: There's no room for flexibility, and repetitive tasks are performed manually. For years, the InfraOps team has trusted manual ways of working and continued with this strategy.

- *Limited collaboration with other teams*: Requests are submitted through tickets and emails; there are dependencies; and delays are expected.

- *Siloed specialization*: This approach has I-shaped expertise, leading to an increase in hand-offs and affecting customer expectations.

- *Highly customized on-prem environment*: Manual efforts are needed to set up new infrastructure or make changes to existing infrastructure. Manual checklists are followed to track the changes. Both integration and architecture are complex.

- *Ticket-based communication*: There are multiple approvals and hand-offs needed when implementing a change, thereby increasing wait times.

Need for Change

The traditional approach was good until the industry took a shift toward digital. Organizations realized that they could succeed only if they knew their customers well and were able to respond and provide relevant, needed services. This digital age needs new thinking, strategies, and processes, as well as investments in people and new tools and technologies that will help them to optimize. For example, if a tester is empowered to set up a test environment the same day using self-service instead of waiting for two weeks, wouldn't this help in completing tasks ahead of time?

It is not only the speed of delivery pressure that is driving infrastructure operations toward agility, but there are other factors too that are forcing organizations to modernize their infrastructure IT operations such as technology drift, customer interests, global presence, etc. See Figure 2-14.

Figure 2-14. *Need to adopt agile InfraOps*

The drift from traditional to agile operations will benefit teams at various levels and foster a culture of collaboration. It also helps teams stay focused toward one goal: delivering quality services on time. While many organizations have already transformed themselves into agile and DevOps ecosystems, still there are organizations that need to initiate and adopt the new culture. Building cross-functional teams, fostering self-service, and standardizing on tools rationalization are all the immediate things to be considered by InfraOps teams. Even organizations that have implemented DevOps and agile have yet to integrate InfraOps and bring in holistic alignment in delivering

IT services. Since agile InfraOps is relatively new, organizations have not been able to move forward due to a lack of available best practices and ready-to-use solutions and accelerators. This book aims to bridge the gap and provide insights from real-life projects for implementing agile in infrastructure operations.

Summary

IT infrastructure operations teams traditionally have been responsible for managing on-premises datacenters that offer services such as compute, storage, networks, security, backup, high availability, disaster recovery, monitoring, management, etc. Their focus has always been on integrating IT assets and ensuring security and compliance are not compromised. IT infrastructure organizations have also been practicing ITIL, which is a framework comprising best practices that guides organizations on how to serve IT services. These services are standardized and help teams to track and meet SLAs. But with changing times, the rigid processes need to be refreshed, and teams that earlier had limited collaboration with application development teams now have a need to collaborate and offer services in an agile way rather than running things in a traditional way. This change is possible through the principles of agile and DevOps.

In the next chapter, we will start covering agile and DevOps principles before embarking on best practices for implementing these methodologies in the infrastructure operations world.

CHAPTER 3

Introduction to Agile and DevOps

This chapter will introduce agile and DevOps, including its values, principles, and benefits when both work together. The topics that will be covered in this chapter are as follows:

- When should you adopt agile?

- Agile principles

- Agile benefits

- Scaling agile with DevOps

- When should you adopt DevOps?

- DevOps in the product lifecycle

We realize that agile and DevOps complement each other, and their adoption enables organizations to excel and deliver frequently. While agile focuses on continuous delivery, DevOps brings in best practices that can fast-track the integration of the development and operations teams and the adoption of the best practices for agile. So, can we just adopt agile or DevOps? What are the overlaps and integration points between agile and DevOps? How do we implement them together? Can we use agile and DevOps in infrastructure operations? To answer these questions, we need to understand agile and DevOps in more detail.

When to Adopt Agile?

Agile is an approach that recommends, facilitates, and provides guidance around iterative delivery, which is possible with connected teams, open collaboration, end-to-end integration of product lifecycle phases, and continuous work on customer

© Navin Sabharwal, Raminder Rathore, and Udita Agrawal 2022
N. Sabharwal et al., *Hands-On Guide to AgileOps*, https://doi.org/10.1007/978-1-4842-7505-4_3

feedback. Adopting agile is helpful when teams need to deliver a minimum viable product (MVP) in short sprints where customer feedback is important to drive the next change or feature in the product. Thus, development teams gain more confidence and trust from the customers of their product. Rather than releasing once a month and pushing integration testing to the end, the focus is on releasing fast, getting feedback, and providing working software early on in the cycle.

Agile Principles

IT teams have been adopting agile methods that encompass the 12 principles shown in Figure 3-1.

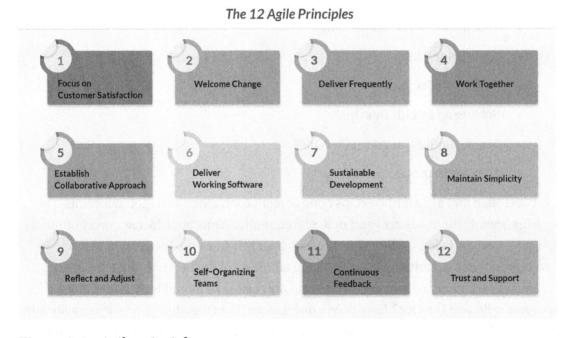

The 12 Agile Principles

Figure 3-1. *Agile principles*

Principle 1: Focus on Customer Satisfaction

One of the key targets for any business is to increase the customer footprint that is complemented with an excellent satisfaction rate. To achieve a good customer satisfaction score, we need happy customers who are looking for products that have flexible service offerings that cater to their needs. This is achieved by staying close to the customer and getting their feedback frequently, which helps IT teams to plan and change course in a timely manner. Early feedback helps teams to avoid large changes later in the process as well. Numerous companies nowadays launch their products in small batches often termed as *alpha* and *beta* versions before the larger, final product launch. This helps them to understand the customer preferences and change the product roadmap as needed. Listening to customer feedback enables teams to build what is needed by the customer and not plan for something that has no votes. Hence, every customer is important, whether it is an internal product team that needs a new environment set up or an external customer that consumes the product or service. A good score is a clear indication that the customer likes the product. This also becomes a key performance indicator (KPI) for teams.

Principle 2: Welcome Change

Change is inevitable, and teams should welcome change at every stage of the product lifecycle. This is possible by coaching teams and helping them understand the purpose of adopting a change. Teams should be ready for changes so that it can meet customer demands. If this does not happen, then the product lags behind the competition, which ultimately negatively impacts the organization. Another way to welcome change is in the initial stages of development where customer feedback helps to alter the course of action in a timely manner. Embracing frequent changes through a simplified process workflow helps teams to be agile. Of course, the end goal is to deliver value to the customer that is achievable when teams share and agree on the mission statement that is driven by the customer.

Principle 3: Deliver Frequently

Customer feedback plays a key role in the product development lifecycle. Requirements are prioritized and changed as per the customer expectations. Modern-day products are delivered in stages, which helps IT teams to understand the actual demand at every stage and course correct accordingly. Each stage needs to deliver working software that is shared with customers for their feedback. This minimum viable product (MVP) enables teams to regularly encapsulate customer feedback and ensure that the product is being built in the right direction. So, instead of delivering an application in months, it is good to reduce the cycle time to weeks or even days. Without frequent delivery of working software, the change required at the end will be massive, and all work accomplished may go to waste. It is also possible that by the time a product is delivered after months of work, the market demand and features required have changed drastically, so the product would work but would not be needed in its current shape and form anymore.

Principle 4: Work Together

Traditionally you will find the business teams and the IT/technology teams running in silos with limited collaboration. The business teams define the requirements, and the IT team builds the product to address those demands. To ensure that the product delivers value, both these teams need to connect and define common goals that meet the customer needs. In fact, within an IT/technology team, there are numerous other teams that function at their own pace (such as the development team, infrastructure team, architecture team, security team, operations team, etc.). Irrespective of their function or hierarchy, all the teams within an IT organization need to collaborate to move toward a shared vision. This is achievable when teams share tools and platforms that follow optimized processes and provide transparency and collaboration. These teams also need to be coached on becoming agile.

Principle 5: Establish a Collaborative Approach

Collaboration is all about teamwork, which is successful through transparent communication. A culture of sharing and collaboration needs to be nurtured in an IT organization, irrespective of a team's location. Teams should be encouraged to share their point of view and practice the notion of accountability. Teams are empowered when they are mentored on agile and they understand the importance of trust and transparency. Teams need to embrace the culture of "pulling work" rather than "pushing work." This is a core agile practice where teams become self-sufficient. There are excellent platforms available that teams can leverage for constant communication and collaboration to address every stage in the product lifecycle. Teams should cooperate with each other to identity hurdles and resolve them as one team rather than working in silos.

Principle 6: Deliver Working Software

The concept of an MVP is essential and should be practiced on a regular basis. The MVP is a product capsule that delivers a specific functionality that can be tested and verified independently. This is successful when teams collaborate to verify the product from every perspective such as resiliency, quality, security, compliance, etc. A working solution is proof that the requirements have been understood and the team has made efforts to deliver it as per the needs. In the initial stages of agile development, teams find it difficult to deliver MVPs timely. There could be various reasons for this such as variance in requirements, incorrect effort estimation, etc. But over the course of time and as the team scales on the agile practices, they deliver MVPs, share them with customers, and look forward to their feedback. This working software should deliver value that was asked for by the customer and that gets incremented over time, which means new features get added as the product grows.

Principle 7: Sustainable Development

Agile development focuses on delivering solution in iterations, and hence it is sustainable over a long time period. Every stakeholder who is connected to the product lifecycle should be able to move with a consistent pace. For sustained development, a healthy work ecosystem is needed that motivates everyone to focus and deliver their best. Teams can practice agility by constantly monitoring their technical excellence to deliver good designs. This principle is nurtured by keeping a check on a team's satisfaction levers and not letting them lose focus. Teams should be able to participate and absorb the expectations and not overload themselves. In fact, they should plan and deliver constant value at regular intervals.

Principle 8: Maintain Simplicity

This principle focuses on not complicating deliveries. The idea is simple: start small, deliver in a timely manner, and increment on top of it. Generally, teams don't have direct access to customers, and they get the requirements from their business team and start building on the basis of these requirements. To simplify the development lifecycle, if the team understands why they are building a feature, it gives them more details and helps them plan better. As they build the product, this will help them stay focused on the core deliverables that provide value to the customer and cut down on gold plating and features that are not required. Using effective tools for communication and transparency helps in driving simplicity. Simple but effective product delivery is what an IT organization needs at the end of the day.

Principle 9: Reflect and Adjust

While the primary focus is to keep customers happy, IT organizations need to reflect on areas for improvement. Organizations that have a defined path to adopt agile should study their ways of working and modify the path as needed on a regular basis. For instance, retrospectives help teams to identify the need for technical trainings to build new architecture or, say, rework on their estimation techniques to ensure that the MVPs are delivered on time. Teams need to absorb the new changes and ask for help if needed to re-adjust quickly.

Principle 10: Self-Organizing Teams

Teams are an important core element of an agile organization. Successful agile teams are those that become self-reliant over time. A culture of ownership and accountability has to be instilled in the organization. This will enable teams to share a common vision.

33

Constant mentorship and empowerment will help teams to upscale and grow, which is achievable by adopting the right technology and platforms that act as catalysts to drive innovation. An empowered team works on a bottom-up approach rather than a top-to-bottom approach. This puts accountability on the teams working on the ground and empowers them to make the right decisions needed to deliver value on time. If a product owner defines the "what" aspect of a product, then a self-organizing team focuses on the "how" aspect.

Principle 11: Continuous Feedback

The success of a product lies in its acceptance. Positive feedback indicates that the product is moving in the right direction and that it meets the customers' expectations. Addressing customer feedback helps teams to prioritize the demands and make changes as they progress. After all, it is a continuous journey of learning and improvement. In fact, customer feedback should be collected at the initial stages of product development so that the feedback is accepted in a timely manner. This feedback should be monitored and tracked so that the customer voice is noted and so that the product roadmap is revisited.

Principle 12: Trust and Support

Two of the most important principles in agile are trust and support. The agile model works when the organization trusts self-organizing teams to take decisions on the ground. Small self-organized teams that can make independent decisions and change course quickly are the keys to success in agile. Successful teams are the ones that are nurtured with new skills and best practices regularly. Teams build successful projects when they are motivated and are empowered to make decisions and are accountable for the value they plan to contribute. Trust the team and provide them with all the required platforms so that they can deliver value. The culture of servant leadership should be practiced in order to avoid complex hierarchical structures that run through rigid processes.

Agile Benefits

Predominantly, agile principles have been used effectively by development teams, and immense benefits have been realized by leveraging these principles. Most projects in the IT space and elsewhere are delivered using the agile approach. These principles are now gaining traction in the IT operations segment where teams are practicing these principles and are also adopting agile methodologies and values. There are four key agile values that help in implementing the agile principles, as described in Table 3-1.

Table 3-1. *Agile Values and Their Relevance*

Agile Values	Relevance	Tools
Individuals and interactions over process and tools	• Self-directed and empowered teams. • Teams perform and participate in the product delivery decisions such as estimation, scope, risks, etc.	• Collaboration and communication tools like Microsoft Teams, WebEx, etc.
Working software over comprehensive documentation	• MVPs delivered in small sprints. • Focus on delivering value.	• Physical and virtual agile boards
Customer collaboration over contract negotiation	• Flexible and adaptive on contractual requirements. • Working with customers throughout on the goal and definition of "done."	• Ceremonies such as product demos
Responding to change over following a plan	• Continuous backlog refresh and prioritization. • Scale and adjust with changes.	• Ceremonies such as sprint planning, retrospections, daily standups, etc.

Scaling Agile with DevOps

As agile software development continues to scale, there is a need to extend these principles with the operations teams as well. This is where DevOps comes to the rescue. As said earlier, agile cannot run in a silo; it needs to be scaled. Applications need infrastructure to run, and that's where infrastructure and teams also need to be encouraged to adopt and practice agile. The development and operations teams together can accelerate the path to value creation and cost savings as product releases are managed frequently.

When to Adopt DevOps?

DevOps is using a combination of cultural philosophies, practices, and tools to increase an organization's ability to deliver applications and services at high velocity. When aligned with agile, it improves team collaboration and productivity. Recent times have resulted in many organizations revisiting how they work and encouraging teams to stay connected and leverage automation to the fullest. Product teams adopt DevOps when they intend not only to connect the development and operations teams but also to look out for integrating processes across the product lifecycle, which is possible by leveraging processes, tools, and automation.

The journey of continuity is an important need for making DevOps successful. The principles of DevOps bridge the gaps between siloed teams and leverage automation for optimizing the processes that connect the entire lifecycle for the product. Each phase in the lifecycle is driven with its own set of tools, processes, and teams. While CI and CD paved the way for integrating in the application world, the elements in the infrastructure world were still running in silos. A DevOps model integrates each phase and each tool, streamlines the processes, and focuses on a common vision—"we build it, we run it." Adopting new tools, moving to the cloud, leveraging APIs, etc., have enabled teams to get connected quickly and share common processes and workflows. And the core principle lies in the belief that this is a continuous journey of improvements. See Figure 3-2.

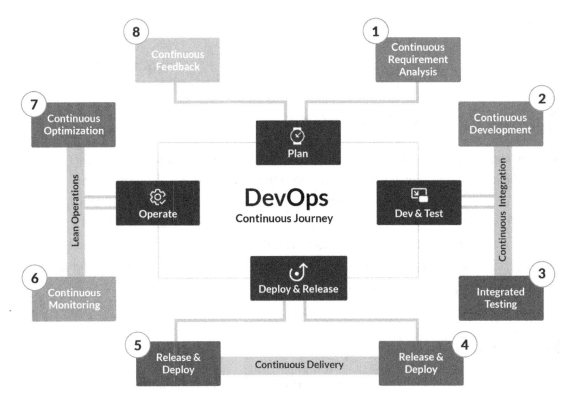

Figure 3-2. *DevOps continuous journey*

DevOps in the Product Lifecycle

Figure 3-3 shows the steps in the DevOps framework.

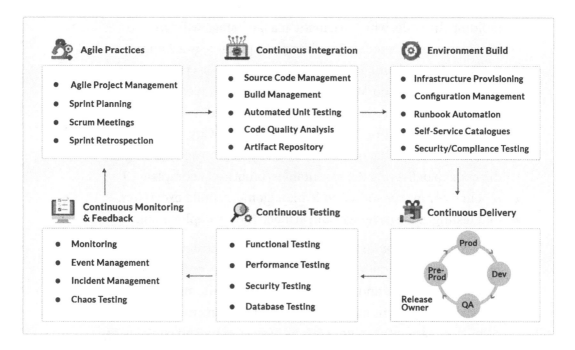

Figure 3-3. *DevOps framework*

1. The *Agile practices in business planning* step establishes business goals and adjusts them based on customer feedback, which helps improve agility and business outcomes. This helps in gaining the trust and confidence of the customers on the value being delivered through the deliverables. This first phase in the product lifecycle is a stepping-stone in building the product journey correctly. With the right adoption of tools and techniques, this phase becomes essential and integrated with other phases. Conducting the right ceremonies, estimating and planning for delivering faster, and embracing the culture of change within the team all play a vital role. This phase is generally managed through tools such as Atlassian Jira, Azure Boards, VersionOne, LeanKit, etc. These tools are extended with other lifecycle tools to get end-to-end traceability.

2. *Continuous integration* is a practice in which software developers frequently integrate their code in the codebase with the code of the application where other team members also add their code. This helps in the early detection of integration defects while building the code, which if caught at a later stage will prove to be expensive to remediate. Building a CI pipeline is a common practice that is running across many organizations today and is a de facto standard too. While this pipeline was implemented in the application space, today it is applicable for building infra pipelines too. Tools like Jenkins, TravisCI, CircleCI, TeamCity, etc., are all well-known tools that orchestrate the key steps, from building the code to delivering the executables/binaries. A complete CI pipeline comprises source code management, build execution, unit testing, code coverage, and artifact/binary deployment.

3. The *environment build* focuses on instant infrastructure provisioning by adopting runbook automation, configuration management tools, and self-service catalogs. Automation in this space helps to reduce IT sprawl. Building an environment comprises various activities such as provisioning and configuring infrastructure, preparing runbook automation, performing and automating security scans, and integrating infra pipelines with ITSM tools. In successive sections, we will be covering examples on how CI is implemented in application and infrastructure space and how are they are integrated.

4. The *continuous delivery* practice focuses on releasing the product across different environments. A well-defined release and deployment process ensures timely delivery of a quality product. Every stage in deployment passes through a series of quality checks. After its success, it is then deployed in the target environment. For example, if the CI build is successful, the CD pipeline picks up binaries from the development environment and deploys them into the test/QA environment. If the CI pipeline is not successful, the deployment will not proceed. Similarly, if the artifacts have to be transferred from the test/QA environment to preproduction, Artifacts will require more quality gates such

as percent coverage that is configured and accepted, security score, etc. Tools such as Jenkins, Azure DevOps, GitHub Actions & Runners, Atlassian Bamboo, etc., are good examples that perform continuous deployment operations.

5.   *Continuous testing* is a practice that means testing earlier and continuously to detect defects early in the lifecycle, which will result in reduced costs. This helps in establishing continuous feedback on the quality of the product. Continuous testing can be achieved by having your test cases automated and executed with each code integration and build process. Testing scope has expanded today, and it is not restricted just to functional, performance, and security testing. As applications are moving toward microservices-based architecture, addressing the growing market needs of the customer base, the need for extended testing has become essential including API testing, accessibility testing, resiliency testing, etc. A few tools in this space are Selenium, Appium, JMeter, HCL One Test Suite, etc.

6.   The *continuous monitoring and feedback* practice involves monitoring applications and infrastructure across all phases and also acknowledging feedback from customers. This will help to lay out actions to optimize and improve the application and thus enhance customer experience and value. Every incident or problem with the deployed application is closely monitored and addressed with agility. ITSM tools like ServiceNow, Remedy, etc., come to the rescue in this space.

So, we have agile principles and a DevOps-connected model that enables organizations to work closely and move faster.

Summary

Agile and DevOps complement each other, but they should not be considered as replacements for each other. On one hand, if agile focuses on iterative development with continuous feedback principles, DevOps focuses on bringing teams together that collaborate with each other and plan for a continuous journey of improvements.

Organizations that practice agile easily transition and extend into a DevOps working model. IT teams that practice agile and DevOps reap long-term benefits such as the following:

- Collaborative and self-organized teams

- Embracing change through trust and transparency

- Faster time to market with automation

- Continuously improving with feedback loops

- Simplified processes and integrated workflows

- Lower costs

- Higher customer satisfaction scores

- Better business alignment

Let's next look at the key factors that are accelerating the transformation of infrastructure operations to agile.

CHAPTER 4

Factors Leading to Agile Operations

In this chapter, we will be discussing the shift toward agile and microservices, deployments, and how continuous testing happens at various levels. The topics you'll learn about in this chapter are as follows:

- The shift toward agile

- The benefits of agility

- Cloud computing

- Microservices architecture

- Deployment patterns and automation

- Shift-left testing

- Changes in architecture impacting operations

Digital organizations are adopting agile operations these days since it has become a necessity. In a May 2021 survey by McKinsey (`https://www.mckinsey.com/business-functions/organization/our-insights/the-impact-of-agility-how-to-shape-your-organization-to-compete`), it was observed that highly successful agile transformations resulted in 30 percent of operational performance that was driven by continuous improvements and removing hand-overs. The survey also measured the agile operating maturity model (for the 2,190 respondents) and its business impact. About 10 percent of the entire sample was driving successful agile transformation wherein agility was driven at scale to create value. The survey also revealed that agile transformation is now becoming a mainstream topic of interest.

© Navin Sabharwal, Raminder Rathore, and Udita Agrawal 2022
N. Sabharwal et al., *Hands-On Guide to AgileOps*, https://doi.org/10.1007/978-1-4842-7505-4_4

There have been similar surveys conducted across different geographies and industries, and they indicate that operating models are getting transformed. But this did not happen overnight. Emerging platforms like the cloud and new software development models like microservices contributed to the need for an agile approach to business. The demand for agility, resiliency, cohesive teams, secured environments, quick turnaround times, digitalization, intelligent automation, and end-to-end integration served as motivators for infrastructure operations teams to adopt agile. See Figure 4-1.

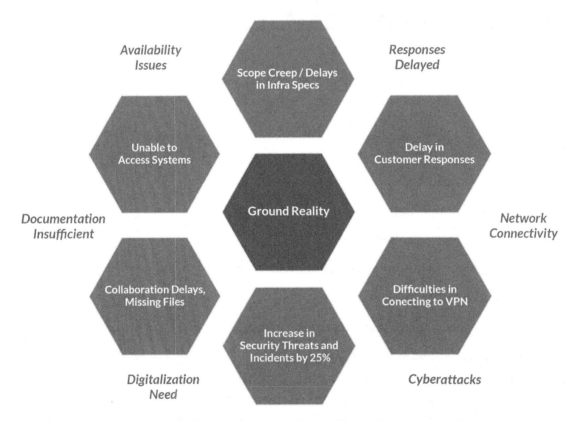

Figure 4-1. *Common challenges faced with traditional operations*

It is true that the vision for an operations teams is to ensure that systems are stable. Traditional ways of working were good until now, but these norms are now set to change in a way that meets and sustains the needs of digital businesses. So, the need of the hour is to shift from traditional ways of operations to agile operations. While the vision remains the same, the underlying ways of working must be transformed. This creates a demand for upskilling our teams as well as introducing and adopting agility and automation for delivering infrastructure services. A milestone-based roadmap will enable organizations to transform from traditional to agile operations. These milestones will include elements of modern technologies like the cloud, serverless computing, or people aspects including building cross- functional teams, creating site reliability engineering (SRE) teams, bringing in observability and automation, and empowering teams with self-service catalogs, which can be consumed through catalogs and APIs. These changes will impact both the "Run the Business" and "Change the Business" parts of IT shown in Figure 4-2.

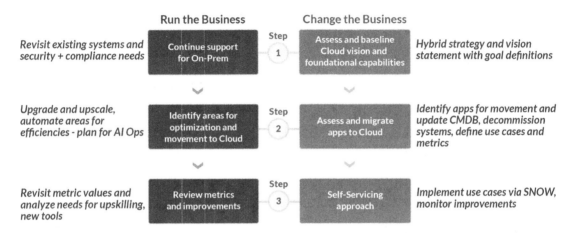

Figure 4-2. *Sample "Run the Business" and "Change the Business" plan toward cloud adoption*

The Shift Toward Agile

The shift from traditional IT operations to agile operations needs to be well-planned and should be re-assessed regularly to measure the adoption rate. It also needs to be tracked on the people, process, and automation fronts. Let's look at some of the key differences between traditional and agile IT operations; see Table 4-1.

Table 4-1. *Comparison of Traditional IT Ops and Agile IT Ops*

Area	Traditional IT Ops	Agile IT Ops
People	Dedicated teams per function/technology	Cross-skilled teams across the function/ technology
	Development and ops teams work independently and work as siloed teams	Development and ops teams closely work together and work as integrated teams
Process	Rigid processes with multiple handoffs	Streamlined processes with limited hand-offs possible with automation
	Incident/ticket-driven approach dependent on manual intervention	Self-service mode of operations
Tools and automation	Limited or siloed automation	Standardized automation framework to drive IT delivery
	Delivering customized infrastructure is time-consuming	Provisioning made faster by infrastructure as code
	Siloed monitoring tools leveraged to scan applications and infrastructure	Integrated and optimized toolset to monitor infrastructure and applications
	Multiple dashboards to track and manage infrastructure services and security	Integrated dashboard with autoremediation capabilities

The transition from traditional to agile is successful in organizations when it has been done in a planned and phased manner. While organizations mentor their operations teams in agile techniques, they are also implementing infrastructure as code and observability technologies. This helps teams to standardize their infrastructure setups as well as restrict any manual intervention; now most of the operations are either fully automated or augmented with automation. Implementing automated systems helps the operations teams to adhere to security and compliance standards.

Benefits That Come with Agility

Working in an agile mode comes with a set of benefits and no side effects. Teams may take some time to adopt and scale, but in the long run, organizations will reap the benefits of adopting agile. Take a look at some of the key benefits that one can derive by implementing the four agile principles (see Figure 4-3).

Agile Principles	Benefits
• Individuals and Interactions	• Integrated Teams • Improved Collaboration
• Working Software	• Self-Servicing • MVP Focused
• Customer Collaboration	• Continuous Feedback • Accountability
• Responding to Change	• Quick Response Times • Streamlined Processes

Figure 4-3. Benefits with agile InfraOps

An important thing to note is that shifting to agile ways of working demands mentoring and coaching for the teams. While automated tools will bring in immediate benefits of self-service and autoremediation, the focus is to streamline the processes and empower teams. So, while agility is helpful, organizations need to look at building a strong service portfolio. This is needed to address emerging technologies such as containers, the cloud, etc. Let's take a look at some of the technology disruptions that have motivated organizations to drive agility across their ecosystem including the infrastructure operations.

Cloud Computing

Cloud computing as a term includes different types of services including infrastructure as a service (IaaS), platform as a service (PaaS), software as a service (SaaS), containers as a service (CaaS), and functions as a service (FaaS). The different offerings have very different needs for monitoring, management, and administration. As you progress from infrastructure as a service to SaaS, the responsibilities of the customer to manage the environment are reduced as the underlying layers are then fully managed automatically by the cloud provider. If you are using Gmail, which is a SaaS offering from Google, you do not need to manage the infrastructure or the application running Gmail; you just consume it as a consumer since all the underlying infrastructure and applications are managed by Google for you. If you were hosting your own email servers using Microsoft Exchange, then the entire infrastructure and the Microsoft Exchange platform would need to be managed by you. SaaS adoption in the email space has actually made on-premises Microsoft Exchange type of deployments negligible because organizations have moved to SaaS. Let's look at the three primary models of cloud computing in more detail, as shown in Figure 4-4.

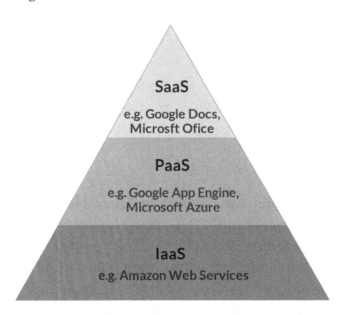

Figure 4-4. *Cloud computing models*

Infrastructure as a Service

In IaaS, the cloud provider provides users with access to computing resources such as servers, storage, and networking. Organizations use their own platforms and applications on top of this infrastructure and manage the operating system and layers above it.

IaaS Features

- Customers do not need to lease datacenters, buy hardware for networking and compute and storage, or integrate all of these elements. The cloud provider provides all these to the customer on pay-per-use basis. The customer gets the ability to scale up and down based on the requirements.

- The customer is saved the work of planning, procuring, installing, and running the infrastructure.

- Since the compute infrastructure is automatically managed by the cloud provider, activities like hands and feet support, datacenter cabling, and networking and hardware failure incidents are no longer required to be handled by the customer's support teams.

Platform as a Service

In PaaS, the cloud provider provides users with a cloud environment where they can develop, deploy, and manage applications without worrying about the infrastructure as well as the platform components. In addition to services provided in IaaS, PaaS provides the operating system, platform abstraction, and automatic management of these components so that the customer can just focus on the application code.

PaaS Features

- The PaaS platform provides a platform for hosting applications and databases; it also provides tools to develop, test, and deploy applications.

- The cloud provider manages the operating system, database, middleware, or other platforms that are offered as a service along with the infrastructure components and security, backup, etc.

- The PaaS platform frees up the resources from customer administration teams and reduces the work involved in configuring and managing access and security for these services using simple and intuitive screens with very less management and monitoring overhead.

- The administration activities of operating system administrators, database admins, middleware, and platform admins are mostly automated and delivered by the cloud provider.

Software as a Service

In SaaS, the cloud provider provides users with access to a fully functional application running on the cloud. Users can authenticate and start using the application on the cloud platform. SaaS could be simple applications like email or collaboration clients or complex business applications like ERP solutions.

SaaS Features

- The entire application is provided to users with a subscription pay-per-use model.

- Since the infrastructure and platform are abstracted, the users don't need to install, configure, or manage these components. In addition, since the application is also provided by the cloud provider, the customer doesn't need to develop, deploy, upgrade, or manage the application.

- The customer can consume the application from various locations, can manage the users and access, and can provide mapping for roles and users so that the authenticated and authorized users can access the required features of the application.

- SaaS manages the scaling of the underlying components like the infrastructure and platform to provide SLA-based availability and response to the users.

- This model involves the least management overhead since almost everything from the infrastructure to the platform to the application development and deployment are delivered by the cloud provider. The application development as well as the operations work are eliminated in this model since a fully functioning application is provided to business and functional users to consume.

Thus, from an agile infrastructure operations perspective, while planning operations teams and processes, one needs to consider the various offerings available from cloud providers. The skills required to manage the environment changes drastically in the different models of consumption. As a customer moves to consuming more SaaS and PaaS environments, the role of infrastructure operations diminishes since the layers are delivered automatically by the cloud provider.

Earlier, infrastructure operations had technical challenges, and the infrastructure cloud computing offerings were not available. Thus, it meant a lengthy process of procuring, installing, configuring, and testing these systems was necessary. Any new application portfolio was taken up as a project that involved teams from the IT infrastructure, procurement, security, facilities, and application teams. Even within IT infrastructure, there were many elements to be considered while setting up a datacenter, such as selecting a colocation facility to host your datacenter and network, storage, compute, and virtualization systems along with connectivity and security appliances. There was also additional complexity involved in ensuring that all these systems from different vendors were compatible with each other, and the integrations needed to be tested before the infrastructure can be made available to the application teams.

All these technical limitations necessitated detailed granular planning rather than iterative implementation as changing anything later would involve a lengthy process of selecting the product, procuring it, and getting it physically delivered and installed, which took weeks. As an example, if there was a design change to reflect higher availability components, you needed two HBA cards, and if you had ordered one HBA card for your compute devices, then you had to order a physical card that would then be procured and shipped by the hardware vendor. Similarly, any changes on network equipment or storage equipment would mean procurement, shipping, and physical implementation of the hardware. To avoid such issues, the IT infrastructure teams evolved processes and systems that required robust and granular planning to ensure nothing was missed in projects. Any changes to the IT infrastructure once deployed would also go through a detailed planning and change control process since there were so many components working in tandem to provide the IT infrastructure, and any change in configuration in one may impact the integration. Thus, the agile processes that got readily embraced for software development were not feasible in the pre-cloud era because IT infrastructure dealt with physical infrastructure elements and there were too many integrations to take care of.

With the advent of cloud computing, all this changed. Infrastructure became programmable through APIs, and the integration of components was guaranteed to work by the cloud provider since the abstraction layer of the control plane and cloud management software from the cloud vendor handled all these aspects. See Figure 4-5.

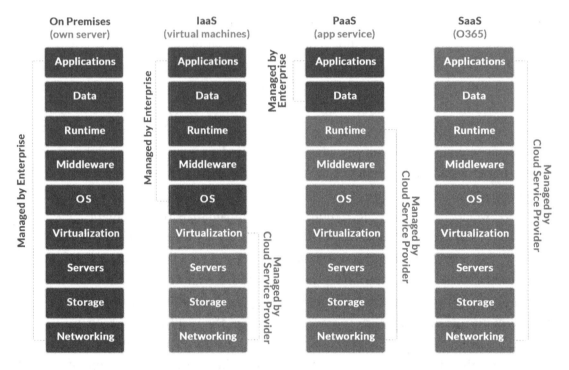

Figure 4-5. *On-premises versus cloud computing types*

Extensive planning to calculate capacity for your environment was no longer needed as any additional capacity could be easily spun up in the cloud environment on demand.

The changes in the technology landscape brought about by cloud computing fundamentally changed the way IT infrastructure was designed, implemented, and consumed. The processes and systems that were set up over decades for IT infrastructure would now need to change because the technology disruption brought about by the cloud changed the game.

Cloud computing brought standardization of environments, configurations, integrations, and best practices. Unlike the past where everyone had to figure out their own best practices, controls, and standards, cloud providers provided best practices, use cases, and standardized architectures that could be used out of the box. The most challenging aspects on networks—setting up the hardware, virtualization software, perimeter security, and security devices—were all available now with the click of a button in the cloud environment. Even if you missed something in the design, you could quickly incorporate changes into the environment unlike in the past. Another fundamental change that took place with cloud computing was the fact that infrastructure became programmable, which meant that the application development teams could use infrastructure elements through code and spin up and down environments through their CI/CD tools and reduce the dependency on the infrastructure operations teams. However, this would mean that soon every application team would have their own cloud environments with the provider of their choice using technologies that they wanted to consume, and there would be no standardization across the organization on the infrastructure and cloud environments.

Since you can consume as much as you want on the cloud environment, there were scenarios where application teams could spin up the environment or use infrastructure and run up cloud computing bills without budgetary and governance controls. Security, compliance, governance, and FinOps disciplines are needed from a cloud computing perspective to ensure that the cloud utilization by the application and infrastructure teams is done in a controlled and secure manner, not in a free-for-all model where application teams could do whatever they want.

Thus, the role of infrastructure teams needed to change in response to the technology disruption brought about by cloud infrastructure.

Microservice Architecture

The new digital and cloud applications are being developed using microservice architecture and running on container management platforms like Kubernetes. Kubernetes has become the most popular open source platform for container orchestration. The container orchestration platform automates the container's lifecycle, from deployment to retirement. The application deployment on the container platform happens through configuration files and can be automated using deployment tools.

The Kubernetes infrastructure is built on top of a cluster that is a set of machines; these can be physical or virtual machines and are called *nodes*. Workloads/applications are deployed onto a cluster. The master node controls the set of worker nodes and provides the management plane functionality. This includes the API server and other components that manage the nodes.

In the Kubernetes architecture, a *pod* is a logical collection of one or more containers that can be spread across multiple nodes as well. A pod packages application containers, storage, network, and other configurations required for running the containers. A pod can horizontally scale out, which means that the application component as part of the pod also scales out. This makes the microservices applications more scalable. See Figure 4-6.

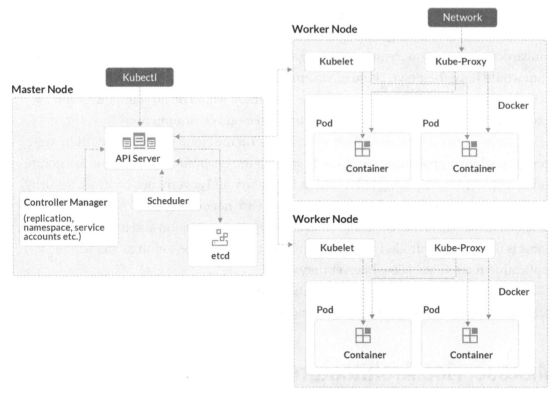

Figure 4-6. *Kubernetes sample architecture*

The advent of microservices architecture and container-based infrastructure poses new challenges for agile operations and DevOps. In the pre-cloud and container era, the infrastructure development and application development were dependent on each other. DevOps emerged as a discipline to bridge the gap between the application development and operations teams. Though DevOps solved the problem from a people and process perspective, the technology aspect was still a challenge. An application deployed into production might have faced issues because the configuration of a production deployment was different than the development or test deployment or some small change in the infrastructure configuration rcsultcd in application availability or performance issues. The other challenge was that the infrastructure and operating systems needed patching and updates every now and then. As an example, for Microsoft Windows, a monthly patch cycle is needed. When servers and infrastructure are patched, it may result in issues in application that require extensive collaboration and testing between the development and operations teams. This led to the discovery of deployment patterns, mostly supported through automation.

Deployment Patterns and Automation

Traditionally, when an application was ready for deployment, it was tossed to the application operations and infrastructure teams for deployment in the production system. A dedicated time schedule was set, and the identified teams joined the implementation. As organizations moved to the cloud and adopted a microservices-based architecture, developers got access to cloud-native tools that allowed them to think beyond development. The modern tools allowed developers to architect their application deployment using several descriptive templates (most of them running in YAML formats). Additionally, they got access to templates available for setting up core infrastructure elements like VMs, load balancers, scaling groups, etc. So, developers who were earlier focusing only on continuous integration (CI) using tools like Jenkins, etc., extended their CI pipeline to perform continuous delivery, which included moving artifacts from one environment to another (such as picking binaries from the development environment and deploying them to the QA environment). Later, as the CI and CD processes matured, these developers were able to automate the deployment of application until production. This process is called *continuous delivery* (CD). In some cases, new production environments are also set up through the automated pipeline. See Figure 4-7.

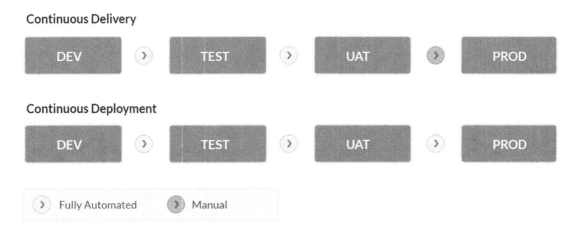

Figure 4-7. *Continuous delivery versus continuous deployment*

With more and more automation, organizations demanded zero or minimal downtime. This was made possible through various deployment patterns that were built using tools like Jenkins X, Spinnaker, etc. Let's look at some of the commonly used patterns.

Blue-Green Deployments

This deployment strategy has two production instances called *blue* and *green* that are isolated from each other. It is the blue production instance that receives traffic. Whenever a new application release is to be done, first that new version is deployed on the green production instance and tested. If this instance passes the test criteria, only then does this green instance get promoted to receive traffic and become the blue instance; then the earlier one gets renamed as green. See Figure 4-8.

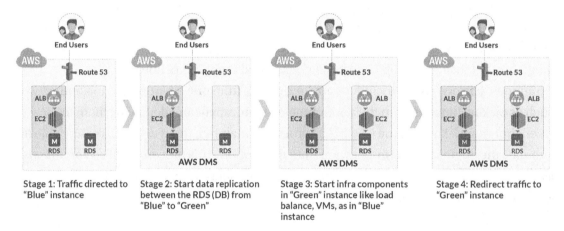

Stage 1: Traffic directed to "Blue" instance

Stage 2: Start data replication between the RDS (DB) from "Blue" to "Green"

Stage 3: Start infra components in "Green" instance like load balance, VMs, as in "Blue" instance

Stage 4: Redirect traffic to "Green" instance

Figure 4-8. *Blue-green deployment strategy*

Rolling Updates

The rolling updates deployment strategy is also known as a *ramped* deployment strategy. The key idea is to roll out new application instances by replacing the older versions. This approach takes care of issues related to long-running transactions while rolling out the new releases. The older instances are replaced with newer instances in a phased manner. See Figure 4-9.

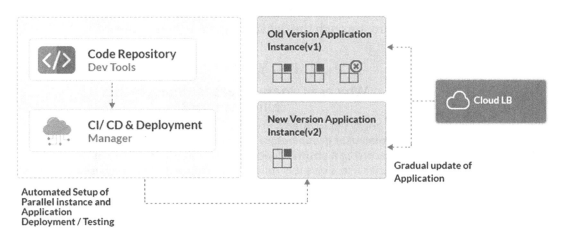

Figure 4-9. *Rolling deployment strategy*

Canary Deployments

The canary deployment strategy, also known as incremental deployment, is like blue-green deployments except for the fact that the traffic to the new application version is directed slowly instead of a sudden cutover. This approach is excellent when teams are performing A/B testing. See Figure 4-10.

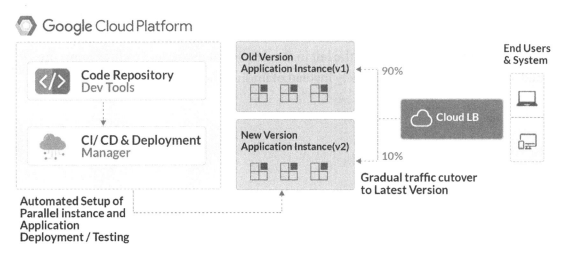

Figure 4-10. *Canary deployment strategy*

All these deployment patterns are easily doable through automation tools and reusable templates. Each of these is well tested through automation test frameworks accompanied by testing tools. Let's walk through the advancements in testing applications and infrastructure through the delivery pipeline. See Figure 4-11.

DID YOU KNOW?

Why are Canary releases/deployments called 'canary'?

Canary deployments are meant to release software to a small user group before launching it on a large scale. On receiving a positive feedback, the release is rolled out to other users else it is rolled back. This technique was used by coal miners where they used the bird canary to test if the mines were safe for humans (since mines often contained dangerous gases). If the canary fell sick, then it indicated that the mines are not safe for humans.

Figure 4-11. *Did you know?*

Shift-Left Testing

Like traditional development, testing often was initiated after the development. While developers performed some form of unit testing, QAs or testers performed functional and performance testing but with limited test scenarios. With the growing demand for microservices, the need for supporting dozens of platforms, and the need to quickly deploy applications, testing had to be modernized. Testing has to be practiced continuously and to be pushed to the left in the development cycle. Product teams are aimed at preventing bugs proactively instead of finding them reactively. See Figure 4-12.

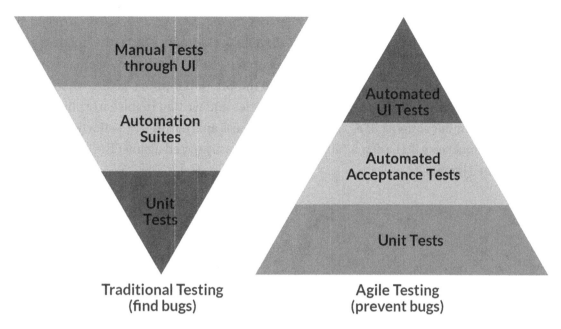

Figure 4-12. *Traditional versus modern testing methodology*

To address the demand, new tools have been invented with more focus on delivering quality code. Product teams pay more attention to technical debt, code, and test coverage. This has paved the way for agile testing and has introduced various forms of testing. Testing is now not restricted to QAs/testers. Instead, business analysts, developers, and everyone on the product team are responsible for ensuring that the product is of high quality with no room for bugs or security loopholes. Let's take a look at the key testing forms that are being practiced across the testing lifecycle of products. See Figure 4-13.

Test every phase in the iteration

	BDD/Unit Testing		Infra Testing		Functional/ Performance Testing		UAT Testing	
Source Control	Unit Test Coverage	Code Quality	Infra Provisioning	Code Deployment	SIT Execution	UAT Deployment	UAT Execution	Prod Build & Deploy
		Static Code Analysis		Smoke Testing		Security Testing		AB/Chaos Testing

Automate to accelerate time to market

Figure 4-13. *Different types of testing*

BDD Testing with Unit Testing: This is a testing strategy known as *behavior-driven development testing*. It is an extension to test-driven development (TDD) that focuses on creating or developing features that meet the stated goals. This type of testing is often integrated with unit tests. The tests are written in the Gherkin format ("given, when, then" format) and are associated with the user stories and written in the early phases. Tools like Cucumber support BDD and enable business analysts to write effective BDD/acceptance tests that are readable and can get easily tested against the expected behavior. See Figure 4-14.

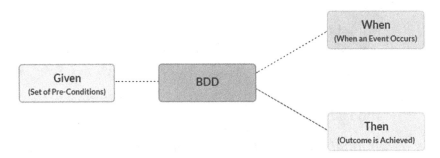

Figure 4-14. *BDD testing*

Unit testing, at times called *white-box testing*, is where the developers test each functionality that they have coded. The unit tests are easily built once the BDD tests are defined. Developers leverage a number of frameworks like JUnit, Nunit, PyUnit, etc., to construct unit test cases and identify code that needs to be refactored.

Static Code Analysis

This type of testing is performed to analyze the quality of code written against a set of predefined rules or standards. Commonly used tools like HCL AppScan, SonarQube, Coverity, etc., enable developers to integrate static code analysis with the application build. These tools generate dashboards that reflect code complexity, code coverage, percentage of duplicates, overcomplicated expressions, and technical debt. See Figure 4-15.

Figure 4-15. *Static code analysis with SonarQube, Dashboard view*

Infrastructure Testing

Infrastructure testing verifies whether the application works with the intended hardware and network. The aim is to test the infrastructure between different environments whenever the new software is ready for deployment. This helps to mitigate risks during migration and production movement of workloads. This type of testing is also performed when infrastructure-related activities are to be performed such as patching, addition of new devices, etc. Various methodologies are available that enable product teams to perform infrastructure testing such as client-server infrastructure testing, network-level testing, cloud testing, etc. See Figure 4-16.

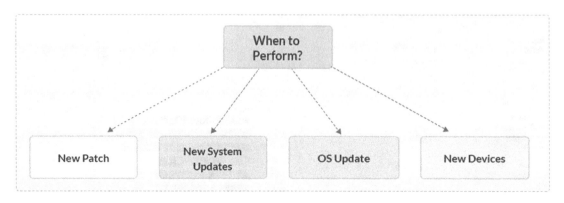

Figure 4-16. *Examples of infrastructure testing*

Smoke Testing

Smoke tests are generally used in integration, system, and acceptance testing where major product functions are tested randomly but are not covered in depth. The intention is to test if the software deployed is running or not. Hence, it is also known as *confidence testing* or *build verification testing.* This testing is performed by the QA testers when the application is released to the QA/test environment, and the process can be manual or can be automated. If these smoke tests pass, then the QA testers may proceed to functional and resiliency testing and, in the case of failures, notify the development team that the build has failed. See Figure 4-17.

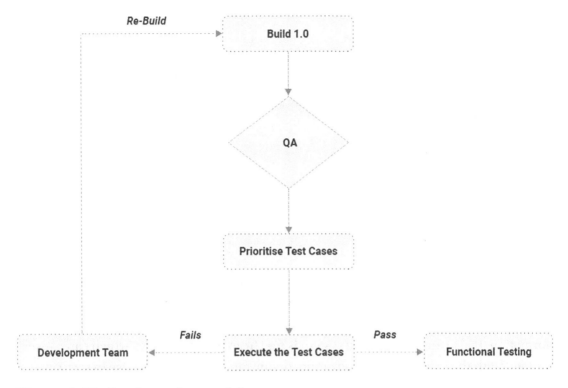

Figure 4-17. *Smoke testing workflow*

Functional and Performance Testing

This form of testing has been in practice for quite a long time where QA testers test the application against its functionalities and performance. This is known as *black-box testing*. This is a type of testing is where the QA department has no clue on how the application has been developed. The testers have a list of test scenarios and test cases that are executed either manually or using automated tools, and the results are specified as pass or fail. Commercial tools such as HCL's OneTest (an integrated suite for functional, performance, service virtualization, and API testing), HP UFT (unified functional testing), HP LoadRunner, or open source tools like Selenium, JMeter, etc., are commonly used. See Figure 4-18.

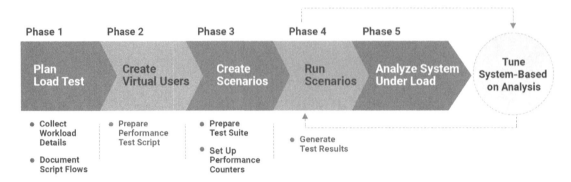

Figure 4-18. *Developing performance testing suites*

Security Testing

This testing category uncovers vulnerabilities in the system and determines that the data and resources of the system are protected from possible breaches. It focuses on finding all the possible loopholes and weaknesses of the system that could lead to loss of information. It also ensures that the system is free from threats or risks, which can cause data loss. With the increase in digitalization, organizations have seen a rise in security threats and hence are investing in various software solutions that proactively scan for such threats and provide these vulnerabilities to the teams on time. There are different forms of security testing that are performed at various levels by different specialists to ensure that the product getting released is tested well, and when it goes live, it continues to monitor the system as well. Tools such as Nessus, HCL AppScan, Qualys, Veracode, etc., are some of the commonly used tools in this space. In fact, this type of testing is introduced in infrastructure as code pipelines wherein security scans are automated to avoid manual checks. For example, the image hardening process requires a compliance check, a process wherein organizations harden a VM image comprising the organization's compliance ruleset. This is done since organizations do not allow the use of VM images directly from the Internet in order to avoid any security issues; this can easily be automated using the existing security tools. If all goes well and the pipeline gets an approval from the security team, the image is moved to a shared gallery, which is accessible to everyone within the organization. See Figure 4-19.

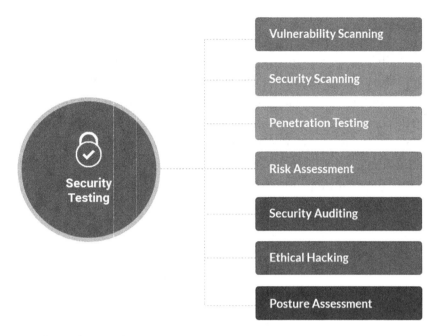

Figure 4-19. *Security testing types*

User Acceptance Testing

User acceptance testing (UAT) is another form of testing that is performed by end users. This is done just before the actual launch in production. The actual users are given access to the new setup to verify the application functionality based on their real-world scenarios. A UAT environment is made ready for the end users to perform this testing with the new application version. The UAT testers have their own set of test cases that are executed in this environment, and the results are recorded. If the user acceptance tests pass, then the end users or the customers provide sign-off for the actual deployment in production; otherwise, the product team is notified for taking steps to improvise. See Figure 4-20.

Figure 4-20. *UAT testing phases*

Chaos Testing

A new form of testing was conceptualized by Netflix in 2011 through its testing tool called Chaos Monkey. The aim of this testing was to test infrastructure resiliency. This helps teams to check whether their existing infrastructure can scale and recover in case of any failures. The concept relies on proactive identification of issues so that outages can be avoided. This testing type is also termed *chaos engineering*, and there are a number of tools available that enable teams to introduce chaos in the system and monitor the behavior. Such an analysis helps teams to build better systems. See Figure 4-21.

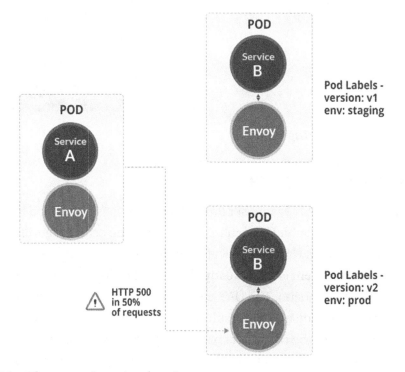

Figure 4-21. *Chaos engineering/testing*

A/B Testing

Also known as *bucket testing* or *split-run testing*, A/B testing is a random experiment done on two variants of the application. The term *A* refers to the control or original variant, and the term *B* refers to the new variation. The version that indicates a positive business impact will be the actual winner. This enables product teams to optimize their web application or websites and increase ROI. Thus, using statistical data, teams analyze the performance of their website and define ways to optimize it based on visitor behavior. As a simplistic example, if 50 percent of visitors visit the variant and this A percent derives more sales than the other variant, then variant A is the winner. See Figure 4-22.

Figure 4-22. *A/B testing*

Ideally, product teams should practice testing at all levels right from the product inception. There are tools available that automate these testing categories, which speeds up agile development. Even in infrastructure as code, teams develop scripts, leverage coding guidelines, check for technical debt, and automate whatever comes their way to enable faster time to delivery.

Changes in Architecture Impacting Operations

Another aspect that has led to the need for agile operations is the change in common architectures. To handle configuration changes, the infrastructure and platform world has moved to a model of idempotency. Simply put, it is an operation that produces the same result no matter how many times it is performed. In this model, tools like Puppet and Chef produced configurations created in scripts that are applied on the servers and endpoints. If any change was made to the configuration at an individual server level or endpoint that is not authorized or initiated through the configuration management tool, the tools agent would simply revert the configuration to the desired state that was assigned to that server based on the role that the server may be performing in the architecture. Thus, a web server role has a desired state configuration, and it won't change unless the desired state configuration is modified for that role through the configuration management tool. This greatly reduces the incidents arising out of misconfigurations or configuration conflicts between development and production systems. This also brings in standardization so the operations team will know what to expect for the configuration of a particular server. Changes to configuration become simpler and automated, and incidents due to changes are drastically reduced in this model. However, one still needs to maintain the desired state configurations and keep the servers updated based on the patching, security, and compliance needs.

With the advent of containerization and microservices, the concept of idempotency has given way to the concept of immutable infrastructure. Immutable infrastructure simply means infrastructure that does not change, so you do not update or upgrade the containers but rather shut them down when there is an update and bring the other containers up. With orchestration and automation coupled with DevOps practices, you can release using a canary deployment or blue-green deployment, and this model becomes easy to use without the overhead of managing the configurations. Containers can be spun up and down in seconds, whereas virtual machines would take a few minutes to boot up. The containers are lightweight and do not carry the overhead of the entire operating system and thus enable the realization of the idea of immutable infrastructure.

Virtual machines are more like pets. Containers are more like cattle. We love our pets and name them and maintain them, and we have a long-term relationship with our pets. This is synonymous with the virtual machines and idempotent infrastructure, which needs to be maintained, kept up-to-date, and the instances kept live for a long time. While containers are more like cattle, they are ephemeral. With containerization and the concepts of agility, high availability, and scalability, the application development and deployment models are rapidly moving toward a "cattle" mindset from a "pet" mindset. A container image is just replaced with a new updated image rather than updating the older images.

Another important aspect that has implications for agile operations is that the container-based applications and architectures are easily portable across cloud environments since they are delinked from the underlying infrastructure components. An application currently deployed on AWS can be easily ported to Google Cloud or Azure without requiring modifications. Thus, configuration dependencies that existed between applications and infrastructure no longer exist in these models. Kubernetes' excellent abstraction over the infrastructure means that infrastructure and development teams can focus on their own areas of expertise.

Thus, the infrastructure teams can focus on things like datacenter infrastructure, network infrastructure, storage infrastructure, cloud infrastructure, cluster infrastructure, capacity management, monitoring, disaster recovery, and security. Application teams can focus on developing applications, building container images for deployment and configuration, etc.

The dependencies and processes that existed earlier where the application teams had to coordinate with different teams to get the job done and wait for infrastructure and right configurations are suddenly gone in the new model. Infrastructure just exists for the application teams behind the scenes to be orchestrated and controlled through YAML scripts.

Thus, the roles and responsibilities of the application team and infrastructure team have changed in the new model. Someone has to deploy the applications using manifest files (YAML scripts usually) and manage new tools and technologies like Kubernetes, Terraform, etc. There are various ways in which teams can be structured to accomplish this end objective.

Mature organizations are moving to infrastructure as code where the configuration of cloud and container environments are represented as scripts and entire cloud environments can be created and destroyed with software code. The changes to the infrastructure world are massive. From using GUI-based screens to writing configuration and automation scripts, the role of the infrastructure administrator has been completely transformed in the new model.

Summary

While traditional operations were successful, the advent of the cloud, microservices, CI/CD, shift-left testing, and infrastructure as code have forced organizations to move toward agile operations. Infrastructure operations cannot live in silos; it has to collaborate and change with new technologies. Agile frameworks that worked well in the development space are being implemented in the infrastructure space too. Teams using ITSM are moving toward agile ITSM frameworks. The transition to the new model is an important step that organizations need to consider, plan, and execute so that no team in the new operating structure is left behind. Before we understand how to get started and move toward agile operations, we should first look at the different agile frameworks and methods.

CHAPTER 5

Introduction to Agile Methods

In this chapter, we will discuss widely used agile methods in detail including best practices, roles, artifacts, metrics, and ceremonies. The topics that will be covered in this chapter are as follows:

- Scrum

- Kanban

- Scrumban

- Comparison of Scrum, Kanban, and scrumban

Scrum

In the traditional infrastructure working model, the infrastructure team was in charge of the operational tasks, which were all manual. These tasks were repetitive and followed the same steps for their resolution every time. Environment building or decommissioning activities were considered as projects that came as requirements in a form of templates. Multiple meetings were required with stakeholders to finalize the requirements. It took weeks to build the servers with all the required configuration because different skills from individuals were required to complete their tasks and there was not much coordination because people were part of different teams and each team had its own set of priorities. Moreover, the requirements kept changing when a lot of rework was needed. All kinds of planned activities were considered to be projects. There was a need for faster delivery along with changing customer expectations.

In the new working model, infrastructure operations teams not only are caretakers of the systems and environments but are also responsible for introducing automation and streamlining processes for development teams. The requirements are called *epics*,

© Navin Sabharwal, Raminder Rathore, and Udita Agrawal 2022
N. Sabharwal et al., *Hands-On Guide to AgileOps*, https://doi.org/10.1007/978-1-4842-7505-4_5

which are further broken down into *user stories* and *tasks*. There are planned, streamlined meetings and set delivery patterns. Teams communicate more and are closely connected. Moreover, entire teams work toward a common goal.

Scrum is a methodology that is well suited for teams that are working on "change the business" (CTB) activities like infrastructure as code. The concept of infrastructure as code (IaC) has been accepted in most organizations for more than a decade now, and it has helped teams to do the following:

- Standardize the provisioning and decommissioning processes

- Track and control the environment builds

- Extend the infrastructure pipelines with development pipelines

- Leverage security standards

- Reduce time to market

Adopting Scrum in IT Ops

The implementation of the Scrum process is similar to the way it is implemented in a development project. Infrastructure teams that are accountable for automation need to plan for its implementation from every perspective. A well-defined strategy that encapsulates people, process, tools, and automation will ensure that the teams learn and scale up quickly. See Table 5-1.

Table 5-1. *Pillars of Scrum*

Perspective	Inputs
People	• Mentor teams on the need for agile practices and their usage. • Identify and plan for new roles in the team (the Scrum team comprises a product owner, a Scrum master, and the team).
Process	• Define the workflow for automating the processes of provisioning and decommissioning. • Identify other infrastructure processes that can be automated.
Tools and automation	• Identify the tool to be used by the team for referring to stories, status, increments, and feedback.

Getting Started with Scrum

The Scrum methodology is a generic framework that can be implemented easily for product development teams as well as operations projects that are deploying infrastructure as code or are automating standard operating procedures through runbooks. The framework has defined roles, ceremonies, and responsibilities that foster a culture of iterative development, trust, and transparency between team members. Sometimes the infrastructure team designates a small team as the DevOps team whose core goal is to strengthen automation and set up infrastructure as code that repeatedly delivers functionalities in small sprints. The team works closely with the business and important stakeholders who share requirements in the backlog that are assigned a priority and that follow the regular agile product lifecycle. See Figure 5-1.

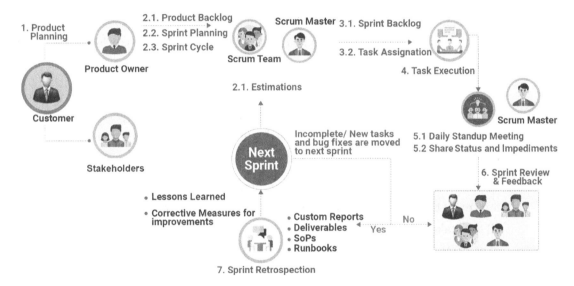

Figure 5-1. *Scrum model*

The framework runs in sprints and continuously delivers value.

- *Product planning*: This is the product backlog creation stage. The product backlog is a queue of requirements that are shared by the stakeholders. In this stage, the customer and stakeholders interact with the product owner and share the requirements. In the agile world, these are high-level requirements called *themes* or *epics*. The product owner understands the asks and states the priority and importance of these needs.

- *Product backlog grooming*: The sprint planning session is where the team picks up the high-priority requirements, provides estimates, and gets started on the sprint. The product owner reviews the requirements with the Scrum team, including the Scrum master. Also, they further details the high-level requirements or epics into smaller units called *stories.*

- *Sprint backlog*: A sprint backlog is another requirements queue that is a subset of the product backlog. At the end of the sprint planning session, the stories are moved to the sprint backlog from the product backlog. The team is assigned stories and meets daily to address the progress.

- *Task execution*: Stories are requirements that are the smallest unit that has to be implemented, and each story has one or more tasks that state the activity or work to be done. Teams update their stories on a regular basis.

- *Daily meets*: This is a daily meeting known as a *standup meeting.* The Scrum master drives the sprint cycle and embraces changes and addresses any team issues. Every day the team meets to share their work status and discuss any risks or showstoppers.

- *Sprint review*: This is known as a sprint demo or review. At the end of the sprint cycle, the work is demonstrated to the product owner, and all the stakeholders' feedback is collected and tracked. The outcome of a sprint review meeting is a "go" or a "no-go" decision of the MVP that is produced. These MVPs could be runbooks, scripts, SOPs, etc.

- *Sprint retrospective*: This is the last meeting of the sprint cycle where the team meets again to study the cycle flow, the stories that were completed and approved, the stories that could not be completed, or the feedback that was shared by the relevant stakeholders. All the lessons that were learned act as inputs for improvisation for the next sprint cycle.

Let's further detail the roles, artifacts, meetings, and practices that are important in the Scrum model.

Scrum Roles

To implement the Scrum methodology in the infrastructure IT ops world, the following roles are needed.

Product owner:

- One who creates, tracks, and manages the product backlog, including the work items needed to drive the infrastructure setup, infrastructure migration, cloud implementation, cloud migration, infrastructure as code type of projects

- Empowered to make decisions for all customers and users

- Shields team from external influences

- Presents and explains product backlog to the team

Stakeholder:

- Collaborates and works with the product owner

- Provides input via the product owner to the team

- Provides a business view that helps the product owner to prioritize the backlog

Scrum master:

- Responsible for maximizing team productivity

- Sets up and facilitates various Iteration meetings

- Shields team from external influences

- Removes barriers

Scrum team:

- Comprised of developers and testers

- Responsible for estimating and committing to work

- Self-organized and cross-functional

- Has full autonomy and authority to run a sprint

- Collaborates with product owner

A typical Scrum team should be no more than eight to ten members. It is important to right-size the team to ensure accountability and easy sprint tracking.

Work Items

A *work item* can be visualized as a deliverable. Unlike in traditional development where a requirement was analyzed, designed, architected, developed, tested, and deployed in one go and followed the work breakdown structure (WBS), in the Scrum world the work items are iteratively delivered and follow the hierarchy shown in Figure 5-2. So, an epic is a big requirement that must be delivered. This is broken down to features and then further to actual requirements called *user stories*, which are linked with tasks. While epics and features can be spread over multiple sprints, stories and tasks are tied to a specific sprint.

Figure 5-2. *Sample requirement breakdown*

Backlogs

All epics are saved in a backlog. These epics and user stories are prioritized by product owner. There are three backlogs: *product backlog, release backlog,* and *sprint backlog.* A prioritized epic is pulled from the product backlog and is put into a release backlog, which in turn will have features and user stories. The sprint backlog is the lowest level, which is a backlog for the current sprint.

Epics and user stories stay in the backlog until they are prioritized and moved into the release and sprint backlog as agreed on by the product owner and the team. Once we have them in the release backlog, we start estimating on the delivery timelines. Story points are assigned to the user stories, which are a measure of the amount of work that needs to be done to accomplish the story. There are many ways of doing story point estimation such as planning poker, T-shirt sizing, etc. We will cover these in detail in Chapter 8.

Scrum Sprints

The first phase to start with in the Scrum project is the discovery phase. This is the phase where project requirements get discussed and user stories are being written in parallel to get an initial confirmation on them. After the discovery phase, the sprints get started.

When we talk of sprints, it is a 3-4-3-week fixed iteration that has a sprint goal to be achieved by the end of the sprint. You can also understand them as an iteration. In a development team, each sprint could be delivering application functionalities like in sprint 1 the goal may be to launch the basic cloud platform features and in sprint 2 the goal may be to add new functionality like security and compliance on the cloud. So, with subsequent sprints, the platform grows and offers more features and capabilities. The question on which functionality goes first is answered by the product owner and the stakeholders who are in constant touch with the customers. Compared to a development team sprint delivery for infrastructure as code, the team will involve delivering the infrastructure setup in iterations/sprints, like in sprint 1 the goal may be to autoprovision test environments with the minimum specifications on a particular cloud. For sprint 2 the goal may be expanded to cover the autoprovisioning of test environments with custom specifications on multiple clouds and so on. Thus, the idea is to deliver working features that are well tested and deployed. Since infrastructure projects are different than application projects, the size of the Scrum team and the duration of a sprint are areas that may differ from the way application development teams are organized in Scrum. Because of a lack of empirical data, it is prudent for organizations to take the recommendations and tweak them to suit their needs based on the kind of projects getting implemented. In general, the infrastructure as code type of projects will align more or less to software development project sprint cycles and team sizes; however, the more complex infrastructure projects may require tweaking of the team size, skills, external expertise, and sprint cycle.

Sprint Ceremonies

Each sprint has four ceremonies that it follows.

- The first ceremony is the *sprint planning meeting*. This is the meeting where the sprint scope gets finalized. It defines which stories will get picked up based on the total story points that the team can accomplish based on its available bandwidth. The artifact that gets defined in the meeting is a backlog, which lists the user stories for the sprint. The product owner must be present along with the Scrum master and team.

- The second ceremony is the *daily standup meeting*. This is a daily 15-minute meeting where entire team participates and answers three powerful questions: What did they accomplish yesterday? What do they plan to do today? Do they have any blockers? This helps in bringing transparency in the team and gives a sense of ownership and motivation to achieve the sprint goal. The product owner need not attend every day but can join in when needed. The Scrum master and team participate in the meeting.

- The third ceremony is the *sprint demo* or *sprint review*. The sprint product or increment is presented to the product owner by the team. This is a time to get a feedback if the team could not get it earlier.

- The fourth and last ceremony is the *sprint retrospective*. This is a time where the team reflects on what went well, what did not go well, what could have been done better, and action items. This helps the team to improve in the next sprint.

Information Radiators

The way we track and control in other SDLC models, we do the same in agile as well. *Information radiators* are used for tracking the status of the release and sprints. Let's see some of the useful information radiators:

- *Scrum boards* visually display the progress of the user stories and tasks associated with the current sprint cycle. They are also used for effective communication and collaboration and backlog and sprint planning. See Figure 5-3.

Figure 5-3. *Scrum board sample template*

- *Burndown charts* are used to show work done versus work planned daily. It communicates how many story points remain to be completed. The team tracks story points in a burndown chart to see if planned stories will be completed on schedule. It helps when adjusting or planning any action that needs to be taken to meet the sprint goal. See Figure 5-4.

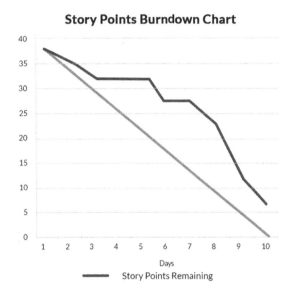

Figure 5-4. *Burndown chart sample*

- *Burn-up charts* tracks it from the other perspective, including how many points have been completed against the goal. See Figure 5-5 and Figure 5-6.

Figure 5-5. *Burn-up chart sample*

Figure 5-6. *Sprint performance sample*

- *Dashboards* depicts all relevant information for the project as a summary. Dashboards are created on an as-needed basis and provide aggregated information and drill-down capabilities. They display the current in-progress information of the project. See Figure 5-7.

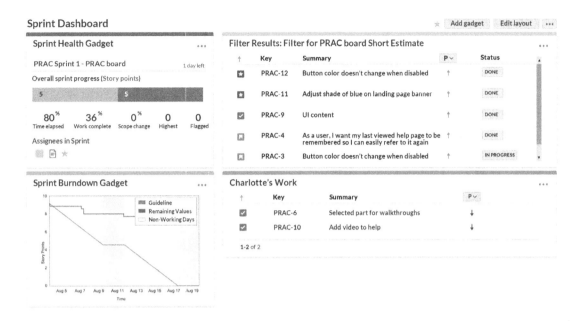

Figure 5-7. *Scrum board example*

- A *velocity chart* depicts the velocity of the completed sprints. This helps in capacity planning for the team. See Figure 5-8.

Velocity Chart

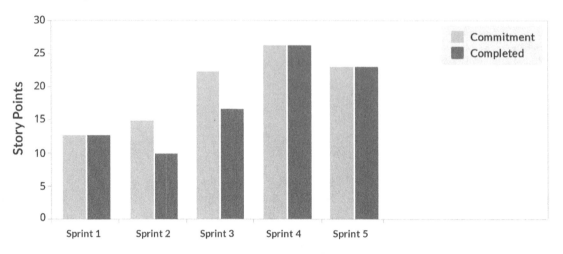

Sprint	Commitment	Completed
Sprint 1	13	13
Sprint 2	15	10
Sprint 3	22	17
Sprint 4	26	26
Sprint 5	23	23

Figure 5-8. *Velocity chart example*

Let's now start with a simple example from infrastructure and cloud operations of creating an infrastructure as code project for provisioning and decommissioning a virtual machine.

Start with creating epics and user stories, which will need to be added to the product backlog in JIRA. See Figure 5-9 and See Figure 5-10.

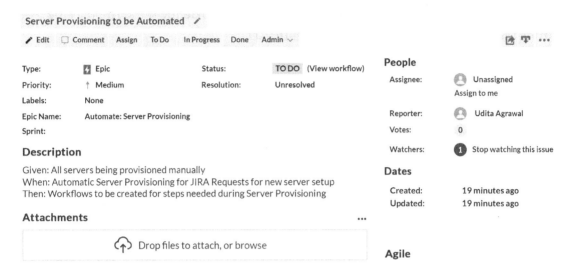

Figure 5-9. *Epic example*

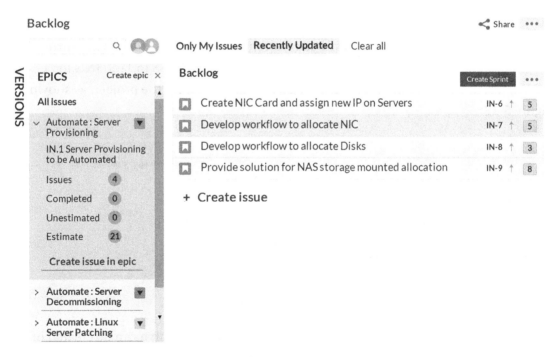

Figure 5-10. *Product backlog sample*

We now have the product backlog, so the next step is to define the sprint backlog during the sprint planning meeting. See Figure 5-11.

∨ IN Sprint 1 2 issues		**Start sprint** Plan sprint ∨ •••
🔖 Create NIC Card and assign new IP on Servers		IN-6 ↑ 5
🔖 Develop workflow to allocate NIC		IN-7 ↑ 5
+ Create issue		2 issues Estimate 10
∨ IN Sprint 2 2 issues		Plan sprint ∨ •••
🔖 Develop workflow to allocate Disks		IN-8 ↑ 3
🔖 Provide solution for NAS storage mounted allocation		IN-9 ↑ 8
+ Create issue		2 issues Estimate 11

Figure 5-11. *Sprint backlog sample*

Sprint 1 gets started, and the daily standup meetings are planned. As the sprint progresses, the items will progress from TO DO to IN PROGRESS to TESTING to DONE, which can be easily seen from the dashboard set up for the project, as shown in Figure 5-12.

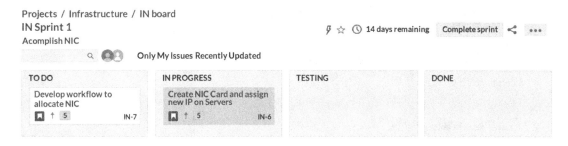

Figure 5-12. *Active sprint snapshot*

Sprint execution can be easily tracked using the dashboards that can be created in JIRA. You can add multiple gadgets in the dashboard based on your project needs. See Figure 5-13.

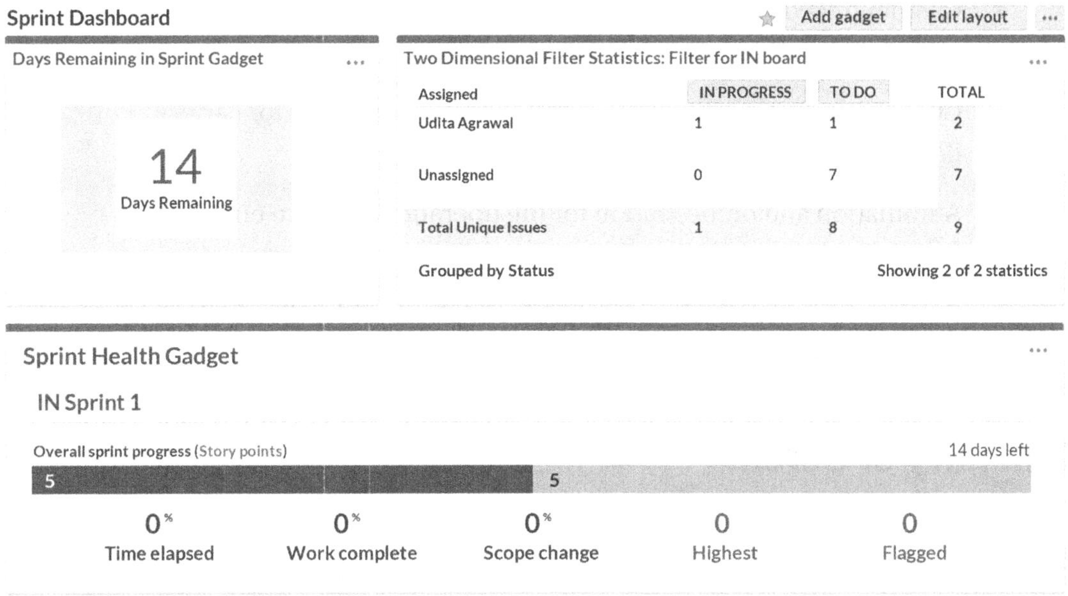

Figure 5-13. *Sample JIRA dashboard*

Along with a dashboard, an information radiator burndown chart is used to track the sprint.

Best Practices in Scrum

Here are some best practices:

- Have a single prioritized product backlog that teams can pull the epics and user stories from.

- Create separate product and sprint backlogs.

- Use common collaboration and communication tools between teams. Tools that enable videoconferencing should be used to establish face-to-face connections among global teams.

- Enable daily standup meetings and frequent collaboration.

- Information radiators like Scrum boards and burndown charts should be used for better sprint tracking and control.

- Customer feedback loops should be enabled in each phase to enable early feedback.

- Continuous testing should be embedded in the process for early defect detection and to ensure a quality product.

- Automation and orchestration for the operations work to enable faster, quality, and frequent iterations delivery to customers.

- Put metrics and maturity assessments in place to identify continuous improvements in processes and delivery.

Summary of Scrum

The agile Scrum processes can be tuned and used in the infrastructure and cloud operations space where teams engineer infrastructure as code and run the deliverables in a sprint fashion. This model of operations has enabled ops teams to work in short sprints and deliver based on priority. Whether it is a network team that needs to upgrade its global network or it's a database team that needs to perform a patch in a phased manner across all regions, Scrum principles can help such teams to switch from old-school ways to modern ways to deliver quickly. Various tools are available in the open source domain and as commercial offerings that can be leveraged to implement Scrum and practice ceremonies such as standups, retros, demos, etc.

Kanban

The word *Kanban* is a Japanese word that means a sign board. This concept was practiced in manufacturing companies like Toyota Production in the 1940s, but its actual implementation in the software industry started in the early 2000s. The key reason for leveraging this methodology was the ability to visualize work items that could be in the form of issues or change requests, etc. In comparison to Scrum, Kanban is an ideal fit for day-to-day operational activities including incident resolution, problem detection, service request fulfilment, etc. Since its inception, Kanban has been adopted by multiple organizations and has also evolved with new practices and variations like scrumban (which is a mix of Scrum and Kanban).

Before we jump into the actual implementation of Kanban for operations teams, let's look at some of the key aspects of this framework.

- Customer ideas are consolidated in a queue or backlog that is continuously churned by the team.

- The framework comprises three key roles that work together to address issues, incidents, change requests, and defects. The request manager interfaces with the customer and prioritizes the backlog items.

- The flow manager works like a Scrum master with extended responsibility to remove hurdles and support the team toward smooth execution and on-time delivery.

- The team is a highly cross-skilled group that pulls work from the backlog and moves it along.

- Each work item entering the system passes through various stages that are depicted as swim lanes on the Kanban board.

- The main goal of using Kanban is to have real-time project visibility that is driven by the team.

- The different stages on the board have limits defined that in turn let the team see the workload and the needed capacity.

- The Kanban framework is good for operational teams that have cross-skilled experts in the team.

- The framework also measures teams' success through a few metrics that are frequently visited, like cycle time, waiting time, throughput, etc. See Figure 5-14.

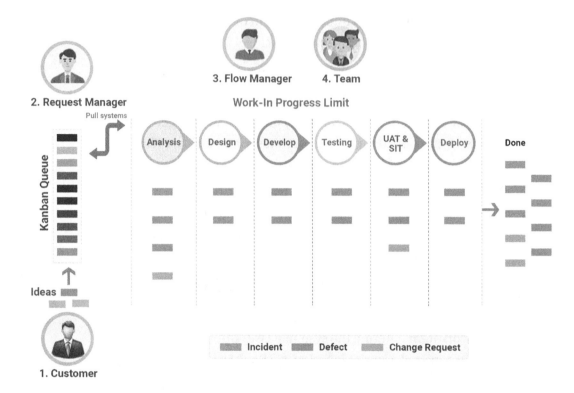

Figure 5-14. *Kanban model*

Let's deep dive into the details of this framework.

Kanban Roles

Here are the Kanban roles :

- The flow manager (in some teams it is also known as the *service delivery manager* [SDM]) is a role that focuses on improving workflow efficiencies. A flow manager ensures that the work keeps flowing, and in case there is a road blocker, they work toward removing that blocker. This role may sound similar to a Scrum master, but it is more than that. In fact, the role is expected to not only track work items but also offer help to team members, make policy checks, and ensure targets are met on time with quality. This role has existed in the traditional IT operations environment, so to upscale this role to an agile environment, all that is needed is the right mentoring for implementing Kanban with best practices. To summarize, the role of a flow manager should target the following:

- Track work flowing in the system

- Remove blockers or risks

- Facilitate change and deliver in a timely manner

- Continuously improve and support the team

- The request manager (in some teams it is also known as the *service request manager* [SRM]) is a role like the product owner role in the Scrum methodology. This role manages the flow of work within the team and drives discussions between different teams and stakeholders. The key expectation this from role is to improve customer interactions.

  - Ordering work items in the flow

  - Owning policies

  - Ensuring governance

  - Tracking risks

- Team

  - Cross-skilled members

  - Pull work from the workflow

  - Each team limited to 15 members

In the infrastructure world, the roles of SRM and SDM already exist, but they follow a rigid process. With a little mentoring on Kanban, these roles will become flexible and will adopt new ways of working. In fact, the ideal situation is that everyone in the team should become an SDM since the goals are to observe the work flowing in, pick up work, and ensure that it is resolved quickly. This is the end state where the team becomes self-driven and self-organized without the need for governance and flow management.

Kanban Ceremonies

Similar to the Scrum method, Kanban teams also practice a few ceremonies that help them to understand the plan, look at their progress, mitigate risks, and prioritize stories as needed. See Table 5-2.

Table 5-2. *Kanban Ceremonies*

Ceremony	Frequency	Purpose
Iteration planning	Monthly (2 to 3 hours)	Review capacity, throughput, lead times
Story prioritization	Weekly (1 to 2 hours)	Revisit backlog and prioritize as per customer demands
Daily standups	Daily (15 mins)	Team connects on risks and plans for the day

In addition to these ceremonies, teams that are building infrastructure as code have a ceremony for demonstrating their MVP to stakeholders. If the demo is approved by stakeholders, then the catalog item is moved to the production environment.

Kanban Boards

The Kanban team visualizes its work through Kanban boards. These boards help teams look at the work flowing in their stream and decide on appropriate actions. These boards are like tables with defined columns wherein each column represents a state, like to-do, in-progress, deploying, etc. Each state represented on the board is called a *swim lane*, and it may have defined limits as well. For example, at any given time not more than four issues can be in the deploying state. This is known as *work-in-progress (WIP) limits*. These Kanban boards are an excellent medium to not only show project status but also put a limit and ensure visibility on the capacity of the team to deliver on the number of tasks/issues that are addressed in a specific timeframe. Figure 5-15 is an example representing a typical infrastructure operations team that manages operating systems. Each swim lane has a name and shows the issues underneath it. While these boards can be manually drawn, tools like JIRA help teams to visualize these boards better. As teams can view the board, they are encouraged to pull work and move them from one state to another. See Figure 5-15.

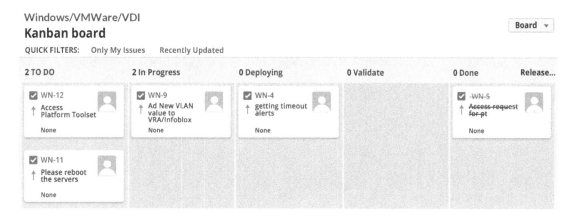

Figure 5-15. *Kanban board sample*

So, the Kanban methodology works on three key principles: visualizing work, limiting work, and iteratively working to improve with self-sustaining teams.

Kanban Metrics

Please refer commonly used metrics for Kanban in Table 5-3 and Figure 5-16.

Table 5-3. *Kanban Metrics*

Metric	Description
Cycle time	Time when the customer submits a request until it gets resolved
Lead time	The actual time spent when the infrastructure IT team started working on that ticket until it gets resolved
Throughput	Number of work items completed per unit of time

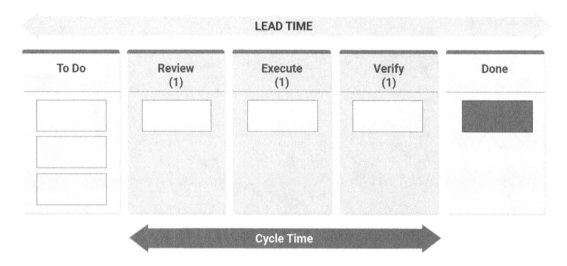

Figure 5-16. *Lead versus cycle time in Kanban*

Getting Started with Kanban

There are various tools that enable teams to practice Kanban. Atlassian JIRA is one such commonly used tool that provides templates for implementing the Kanban methodology. This tool can be installed and used as an on-premises solution or can be used through the cloud offering.

The tool has user-friendly templates to practice Kanban. Each project created in JIRA has the following specifications:

- Workflow

- Name

- Unique key/identifier

Every time a new project is created in JIRA, it prompts for the project template, the workflow to be implemented, and the project name that has a key that is used to identify tickets. See Figure 5-17.

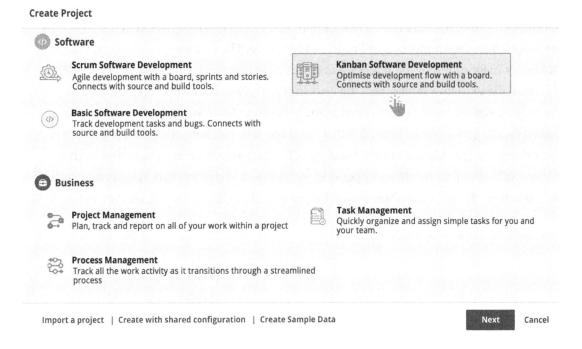

Figure 5-17. *Creating a Kanban project in JIRA*

Each project template is associated with a workflow that defines the journey of a ticket. As beginners, teams can leverage existing workflows, as shown in Figure 5-18, or create a custom workflow that addresses their project needs.

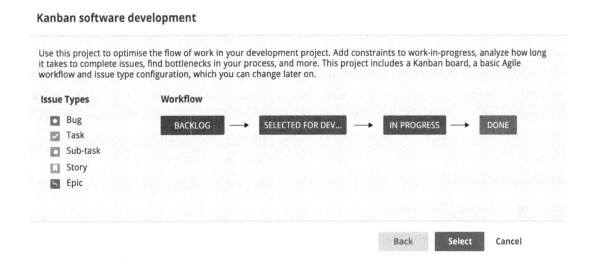

Figure 5-18. *Kanban workflow in JIRA*

The workflow shown describes how a ticket will be placed in the backlog and then how it moves to a different state by the team members. The states mentioned in the workflow are Selected for Development, In Progress, and Done. These states are customizable and can be set in for different issue types like in this case Bug, Task, Sub-task, Story, and Epic.

Once the workflow is selected, the next step is to give a name and an identifier to the project. For example, if the project name is Custom-Kanban-Project, then the tool automatically generates an identifier that is a three-letter abbreviation. This identifier is something that gets tagged to each issue type. For example, stories written now in this project will have story numbers appended with the key. If this were modified with a value like OPS, then the story numbers would be generated as OPS-1, OPS-2, etc. See Figure 5-19.

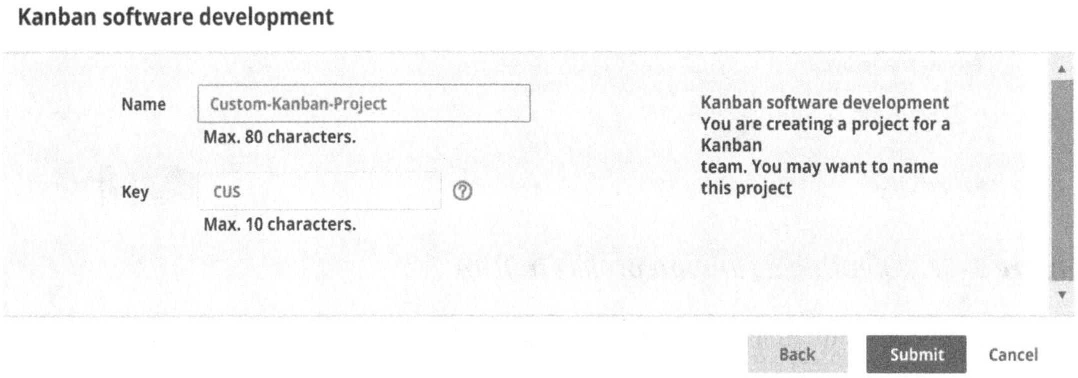

Kanban software development

Figure 5-19. *Naming Kanban projects in JIRA*

It is important that a Kanban project creation is well thought through. If there is a need for customizing the states, issue types, identifiers etc., then this should be done during Kanban practices setup for the project.

Once the project is set up, the next important thing to set up is WIP limits. WIP limits are defined as the team's capacity to address a minimum and maximum number of tasks at any given point in time. This helps teams to avoid overload across all the stages in the life of a story or an issue. Based on your current team size, skillset, and working hours, define the maximum limits for each of the swim lanes. Let's study the process of how to calculate WIP limits.

Steps for Defining WIP Limits

Let's assume that we have created four swim lanes on the Kanban board named Development, Review, Testing, and Deployment. We will set the WIP for each of these four stages, which means finding the maximum number of issues or tickets that can be managed at each of these stages. Before we start with the process of calculating WIPs, first let's divide each stage into two sections that will depict a value-added (VA) activity and non-value-added (NVA) activity.

A VA activity indicates actual work done, and an NVA activity refers to the wait or delay times that occur during work execution. For example, let's divide the development stage into an NVA named "Ready for development" and a VA activity as "In development." The state "Ready for development" indicates a list of prerequisites to be done before the actual development starts, and the state "In development" refers to the actual development state. So, each stage in the lifecycle will have VAs and NVAs, and this division will help us to estimate the right WIP. Divide each of the other stages as shown in Table 5-4.

Table 5-4. *Activities Categorization in Kanban Stages*

Development		Review		Testing		Deployment	
Ready for development	**In development**	Ready for review	**Reviewing stage**	Ready for testing	**In testing**	Ready for deployment	**Deployment stage**

VA activity

NVA activity

With this updated Kanban board, we will now proceed to estimate the WIP for all the VA states. The formula for calculating WIP for a Kanban board is as follows:

WIP = Total Tasks * Time %

Prerequisite 1 is Total tasks = Team size / Efficiency => refers to the maximum number of tickets that can stay on the board. This formula needs the team size (for our example we will consider it to be five) and efficiency factor (which needs to be calculated, described as prerequisite 1).

*Prerequisite 2 is Time % = [VA / Sum of VAs] * 100 => refers to the percentage of time spent on VAs. To calculate this value, we need to find out the VA values for all the states (described as prerequisite 2).*

Prerequisite 1: Total Tasks (Calculation Steps)

Step 1.1 → Calculate the overall efficiency factor.

With the VAs and NVAs chalked out, we will calculate the number of tasks that an engineer can address at the same time. For calculating this value, we need to first find out the time spent for VA and NVA activities for all the four stages and later estimate the efficiency value, which is calculated using this formula:

$$\text{Efficiency} = \text{VA time} / (\text{VA time} + \text{NVA time})$$

The value for efficiency is made up of VA and NVA time values. Let's break down this formula into further steps and calculate the same for our example board.

Find VA and NVA values: Discuss with the team the average efforts spent across all the eight swim lanes. For example, the team confirms that tickets in "Ready for development" swim lane takes one day, but once it moves to the "In development" stage, it needs three days. Document the efforts across all the other phases; Table 5-5 shows the efforts estimated for all the stages as an example.

Table 5-5. *VA and NVA Activity Efforts in Kanban Stages*

Development		Review		Testing		Deployment	
Ready for development	**In development**	Ready for review	**Reviewing stage**	Ready for testing	**In testing**	Ready for deployment	**Deployment stage**
1 day	**3 days**	0.5 days	**0.5 days**	0.5 days	**1 day**	0.5 days	**0.5 days**

VA activity

NVA activity

Sum up the total efforts for all the VAs and NVAs as follows:

Time spent for VA activities from all phases = 3 + 0.5 + 1 + 0.5 = 5 days

Time spent for NVA activities from all phases= 1 + 0.5 + 0.5 + 1 = 3 days

Now, we will find out the efficiency value, as shown here:

Efficiency = VA / (VA + NVA) => 5 / (5 + 3) => .62

Efficiency % = .62 * 100 => 62%

This value is an indication for the number of tasks that an engineer can have at the same time on the board. A board with 100 percent efficiency will indicate that there are no waiting times, and an engineer focuses on only one issue at a time (an ideal situation).

Step 1.2 → Calculate the total tasks.

Now, we know the team size value and have found the efficiency value too. We will now calculate the total task value (the first part of the WIP formula). This is calculated as follows:

Total tasks = Team size / Efficiency

Total tasks = 5 / .62 = ~8 tasks.

This means that our Kanban board at any given time can have approximately eight tasks, which can be spread across different swim lanes, or stages.

Prerequisite 2 - Time% (Calculation)

Step 2.1 → Estimate the time percentage for all the VAs.

To calculate time percentage for all VA activities for each stage we need to use the following formula:

Time % = [VA / Sum of VAs] * 100

We will estimate this value for all the VAs as shown in Table 5-6.

Table 5-6. *Time % Calculation for VA Activities in Kanban Stages*

Development		Review		Testing		Deployment	
Ready for development	**In development**	Ready for review	**Reviewing stage**	Ready for testing	**In testing**	Ready for deployment	**Deployment stage**
1 day	**3 days**	0.5 days	**0.5 days**	0.5 days	**1 day**	0.5 days	**0.5 days**
	Time% = 3 / 5 =60%		**Time% =0.5/5 =10%**		**Time% =1 / 5 =20%**		**Time% =0.5 / 5 =10%**

VA activity

NVA activity

Based on our assumptions, the state "In development" has a VA value of three days. We will divide it from the total VA value, which is five, and the value turns out to be 60 percent. This indicates that 60 percent of the total time is needed or will spent here in this state of the lifecycle. Similarly, we do it or others as well, and you will see that the reviewing stage has a value of 10 percent, the in-testing state was a value of 20 percent, and finally the deployment stage state has a value of 10 percent. On adding all these values, it should sum up to 100 percent.

Calculating WIP

Finally, we calculate the WIP limits for each VA column based on the values derived (from prerequisites steps 1 and 2) in the following formula:

WIP = Total tasks * Time %

See Table 5-7.

Table 5-7. *WIP Calculation for VA Activities in Kanban Stages*

Development		Review		Testing		Deployment	
Ready for development	**In development**	Ready for review	**Reviewing stage**	Ready for testing	**In testing**	Ready for deployment	**Deployment stage**
1 day	**3 days**	0.5 days	**0.5 days**	0.5 days	**1 day**	0.5 days	**0.5 days**
	Time% **= 3 / 5** **=60%** **Total tasks** **=8** **WIP** **= .6 * 8** **~4 tasks/ ticket**		**Time%** **=0.5/5** **=10%** **Total tasks** **=8** **WIP** **= .1 * 8** **1 task/ ticket**		**Time%** **=1 / 5** **=20%** **Total tasks** **=8** **WIP** **= .2 * 8** **~2 tasks/ tickets**		**Time%** **=0.5 / 5** **=10%** **Total tasks** **=8** **WIP** **= .1 * 8** **1 task/ ticket**

VA activity

NVA activity

If you sum up all the WIP values, it comes out to be eight, which confirms our calculation (as per the process defined in prerequisite step 1). Moreover, looking at the board, it becomes clear which states in the lifecycle need more attention. Let's summarize our example for a team of five engineers working in Kanban mode:

- Each issue or a ticket on the Kanban board will undergo four key stages: development, review, testing, and deployment.

- Each of these stages will have some idle time where the engineer will be waiting or preparing before the actual work begins.

- Hence, each stage will have two components: VA and NVA. The efforts spent for each of the VAs and NVAs are discussed and noted with the team.

- We calculate WIP limits for all the VAs in each of the four stages that are dependent on finding values on the percent of time and total number of tasks (WIP = Total tasks * Time%).

- The total number of tasks is calculated as Total tasks = Team size / Efficiency.

- Efficiency is calculated as VA / (VA + NVA).

- Time% is calculated as [VA / Sum of VAs] * 100.

- For our example, the maximum limit for in development is four tasks or tickets, while a review can have one ticket, testing can have maximum two tickets, and deployment can have only one ticket. But, in total a maximum of eight tickets can be worked by a team of five engineers.

As beginners, it's OK to start with the basic values and make assumptions; as you mature these values converge to an efficiency level best suited for your work and team size. See Figure 5-20.

DID YOU KNOW?

WIP limits for NVAs?

NVA columns introduce waste since they indicate wait times and delays and hence one should have minimum tasks in these columns. To start with, teams should have a value of 1 for each of the NVA columns on the kanban board. Gradually as the team matures, this column value should decrease or should move toward zero value.

Figure 5-20. *Did you know?*

Tools like JIRA allow leads to set up WIP limits for all the swim lanes. See Figure 5-21.

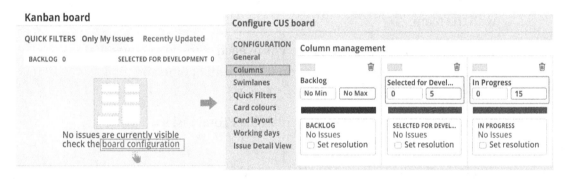

Figure 5-21. *Configuring WIP limits in JIRA*

Let's take another example to see how the WIP limits are reflected in the tool like JIRA and what happens if there are more tasks assigned to the VA columns and they exceed the WIP limits. The workflow state Selected for Development will not have more than five work items in its queue. It's the same for the "In progress" state; the maximum limit set is 15. Now if the number of issues breach the defined maximum limit then, that swim lane gets highlighted in red. For example, say we have an assignment to be done wherein RHEL systems are to be upgraded to a higher version. To perform this project activity, we will create a few epics that are further divided into tasks. Whenever the issues are created, they are placed in the backlog. Team members or leads move these issues between swim lanes based on their bandwidth and the urgency on these issues. Figure 5-22 is a quick illustration of the stated example.

Kanban board

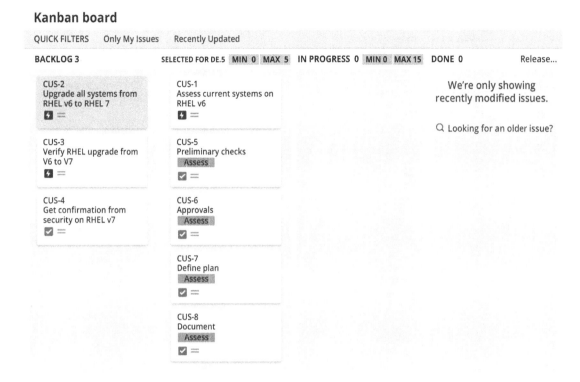

Figure 5-22. *Viewing WIP limits in JIRA*

The Selected for Development swim lane has a maximum limit of five issues, and the moment you drag a new issue from backlog it turns red. This alerts the user that more work items cannot be placed. This is an excellent method to review team capacity that brings in transparency and helps to track and prioritize work. See Figure 5-23.

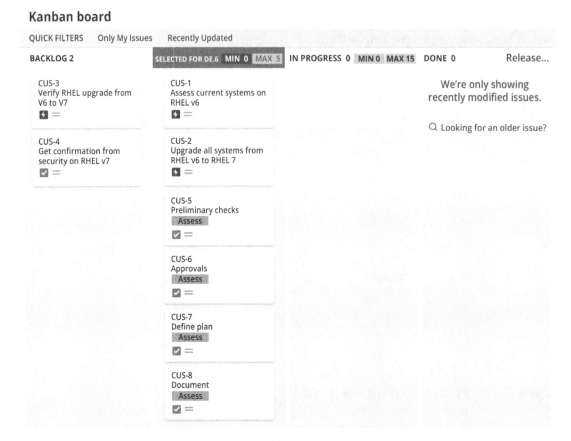

Figure 5-23. *Viewing Kanban board with WIP limits in JIRA*

By defining these WIP limits, teams get to focus on what needs attention and prevent tasks from accumulating at any step. It allows teams to know their capacity as well. This mode of working also highlights inefficiencies and bottlenecks. These values should be frequently revisited to see if they need updating.

In the beginning, the ops teams may have separate backlogs for each of the areas like and Windows, Database, Backups, and slowly as teams mature and get used to these practices, the backlogs and teams can be combined (one common backlog), thus leading to cross-functional teams. As teams upscale, they should also do retrospectives themselves and update their ways of working in case things are not functioning as planned.

While tickets pour into the backlog and get picked up by members, it is also good to create horizontal lanes to differentiate between a simple incident versus an expedited incident. This can be set in the tool by configuring the board. For example, you need to set up two lanes: one that addresses simple incidents and the other that needs immediate attention (tickets with highest priority). Click the Configure Board option to view the swim lanes, as shown in Figure 5-24.

Figure 5-24. *Configuring a Kanban board in JIRA*

Once you view the page wherein you can configure the workflow and related states, select the option to update the swim lanes and mention the lanes and the criteria that differentiates them. See Figure 5-25.

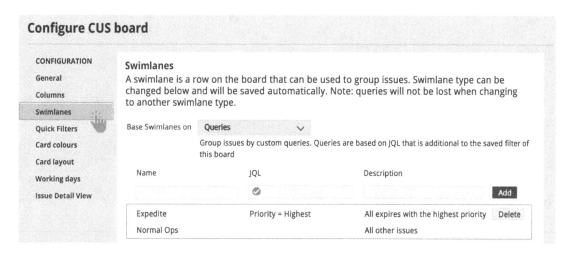

Figure 5-25. *Defining horizontal swim lanes in JIRA*

By default, the JIRA Kanban project offers the Expedited lane; you can customize or rename it or create more swim lanes as needed. For the previous example, we mentioned that the expedited lane will have incidents with a priority value of highest, and the rest of the tickets will be in the other lane. As tickets get created, based on their priority, the tool will segregate the ticket display for teams to view the status instantly. See Figure 5-26.

Kanban board

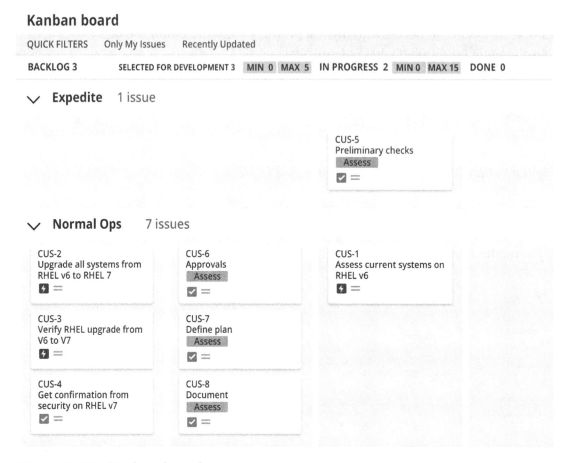

Figure 5-26. *Kanban board status*

Note   Teams can succeed in Kanban adoption when they are comfortable with the basic concepts of workflows, lanes, and types of tickets, and can practice the culture of "pulling" work rather than work being pushed to them. A Kanban board is a dynamic visualization of the team workload and helps teams to plan and work in an effective way.

Best Practices in Kanban

Identify Workflow States Early

For infrastructure IT operations teams that are just starting with Kanban, they can start with just three workflow states: To Do, Work in Progress, and Done. If they plan to build and deploy new infrastructure components or, say, run through patching activities, then they can define lifecycle phases as In-Queue, Design, Coding, Test, and Done. There are teams that also have additional workflow states that mention approval states or wait time. It is advised that the workflow states are well thought through with the team and then implemented. See Figure 5-27.

Figure 5-27. *Kanban workflow states*

Determine WIP Limits

The concept of Kanban is about magnifying teams' visibility and analyzing capacity timing. Finding WIP limits for all the workflow states will benefit the team and help to plan for increasing capacity if need be. There are two ways to define WIP limits. See Table 5-8 and Table 5-9.

Table 5-8. *Method 1: Define WIP for Each Workflow State*

	WIP Limit =2 No of Designers=2	WIP Limit=3 No of Programmers = 3	WIP Limit=1 No of Testers =1	
Not Started	Design	Coding	Test	Done

Table 5-9. *Method 2: Define WIP Limit for Overall Workflow Rather Than Each Workflow State*

	WIP Limit =6			
Not Started	**Design**	**Coding**	**Test**	**Done**

Other Best Practices

- WIP work limits need to be configured to suit a project's current needs, and this should be monitored and updated.

- Lead and cycle time are influenced by the commitments made during the project start. Hence, it is important to track these metrics and take necessary actions to improve them.

- Monitor bottlenecks daily and act actively on them. Encourage team members to speak up when noticing showstoppers.

Establish a release plan that is shared with the team and well-coordinated with the product teams. For example, releasing a patch can be merged with application deployment.

Summary of Kanban

The Kanban model is an excellent fit for infrastructure ops teams that are just getting started with agile and want to transform to a new model of operations. Instead of running operations in a traditional way, Kanban offers teams wider visibility and accountability wherein work is to be pulled by them instead of being pushed. This kind of a working model builds a culture of trust and transparency. Also, this model enables the infrastructure operations teams to analyze capacity proactively by defining work-in-progress limits across the key phases of IT operations. Tools such as Atlassian JIRA offer built-in templates for teams to start using. With the right mentoring and transition to agile tools, infrastructure ops teams will increase their productivity over time.

Scrumban

Scrum and Kanban are the two widely practiced agile methods devised for different team categories. If Scrum was preached by the development teams, then Kanban served as an ideal option for the infrastructure operations team. Both methods individually benefitted teams. But as time evolved and the need for DevOps emerged, IT organizations started looking for a hybrid method, which brings in the best from both methods. This became a prominent ask as development teams started closely with the infrastructure operations team and a few started forming a DevOps team. This led to designing a new hybrid agile method called scrumban, which was coined by Corey Ladas (a lean-Kanban practitioner). This method offers the predictability element from Scrum with the flexibility from Kanban. It is an ideal fit for DevOps and maintenance teams or large-scale projects. See Figure 5-28.

Figure 5-28. *Scrum + Kanban*

Scrumban is a hybrid method that delivers in a continuous manner and accepts changes at any time. It is flexible like the Kanban methodology but embraces the best practices of Scrum as well. This method introduces a new concept called *bucket planning* wherein teams plan the activities and place them in buckets.

- *One-year bucket*: Long-term visionary goals

- *Six-month bucket*: Approved plans

- *Three-month bucket*: Plans ready for execution

- *Current bucket*: Actual plan in action, teams working on tasks

Such a method is suitable for teams who do not want to just focus on the current workloads and performance but also would like defined goals. For example, an infrastructure team practicing Scrumban can have long-term goals like adopting AIOps in the one-year bucket, tool investments and implementation in the six-month/three-month buckets, and actual operational tasks and infrastructure pipeline work in the current bucket. This kind of method brings in transparency since the team can align with the roadmap. This is an ideal agile method for teams where priority changes are very frequent. Let's dive more into this method and understand its key construct. See Figure 5-29.

Figure 5-29. *Backlogs*

Scrumban Roles

There are no defined roles while implementing scrumban. Whatever roles exist can be considered and upscaled to meet the expectations. Every member in the team is accountable for the stories, and this is where the work-in-progress limits also help. Existing roles like Scrum master, product owner, specialists, and the Scrum team all can continue to operate in this model. The only prerequisite is that the team should be enabled to effectively use this method.

Scrumban Ceremonies

The basic ceremony that is recommended while practicing scrumban is the daily standup. Standups are conducted daily to track the progress and brainstorm on any risks that are identified for the current bucket. Teams refer to the scrumban board for tracking WIP limits, and their backlog is driven just-in-time by removing the rigid constraints of sticking to what exists in a product backlog. Additional meetings like planning meetings or retrospectives are planned only if the team feels the need for them.

Getting Started with Scrumban

It is evident that scrumban focuses on goals, work visibility, and process improvements, and of course the key foundation to its success is "the team." It has also been observed that some organizations customize scrumban in a way that best serves their teams. Agile management tools like Atlassian JIRA offer templates for Scrum and Kanban, but there is nothing explicitly defined for scrumban in the tool. Teams leverage either Kanban or Scrum as the base template and then customize the template to address scrumban working methods. A few new tools have recently become available like Method Grid,

Monday.com, ClickUp, Kanban Tool, Favro, etc., that offer scrumban templates along with Scrum and Kanban templates. Most of them are cloud-based applications. So, if teams have licenses for JIRA, then they can leverage them for practicing scrumban; otherwise, they can opt for the new tools available.

One important thing to remember is that the key requirement for enabling teams on scrumban is the "board." This Scrumban board will be the visibility tool for teams for viewing tasks, flagging tasks, and monitoring overall project status as well as viewing what is in store in the near future. See Figure 5-30.

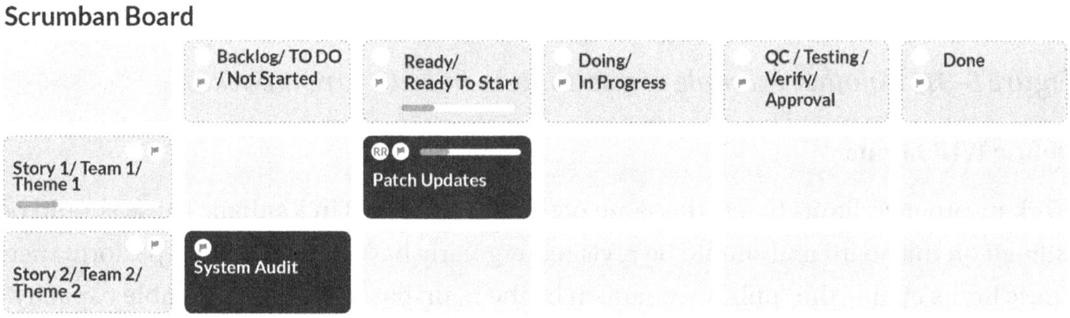

Figure 5-30. *Sample Scrumban board, team-based view*

Assuming you have your choice of tool in place, the following steps are recommended for practicing Scrumban.

Design a Scrumban Board

The board is the most important aspect in Scrumban that will reflect the team progress. This is like the Kanban board that displays stories and tasks flowing between states (like To Do, In Progress, Done). Some teams define states or stages that resemble the transition states defined in the Scrum approach (like To Do, Designing, Development, Verification, Deployment).

This board should display current bucket items that can be further segregated into sections that reflect generic operational tasks versus new infrastructure requests.

The board example in Figure 5-31 shows activities for two teams, one that performs regular business as usual activities and the other that addresses automation of change the business requirements like setting new infrastructure or decommissioning stale environments. There is a third section that highlights ad hoc queries and requests that need to be discussed and planned.

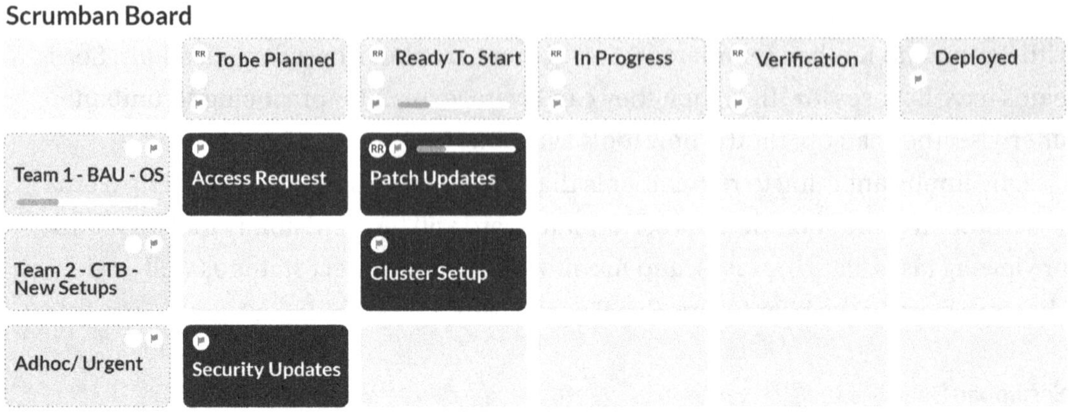

Scrumban Board

Figure 5-31. *Another example of a scrumban board, current bucket*

Define WIP Limits

Work-in-progress limits follow the same pattern as practiced in Kanban. These should be defined on the board and should be revisited regularly based on the team's performance. These limits enable the "pull" mechanism by the team based on their available capacity. For the board in Figure 5-32, there are limits defined for each state.

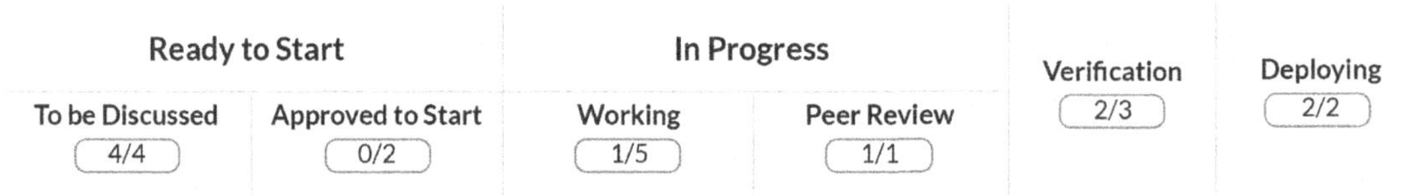

Figure 5-32. *WIP limits on a scrumban board*

Schedule Meetings

Like the daily Scrums, plan for daily meetups with the team. This mode of communication should be focused, with a defined agenda for each day. The team interacts by sharing their workload and risks that need attention. In addition to these daily meetups, teams can trigger sprint meetings for discussing new requirements and prioritizing them. This does not have to be every two weeks. Planning activities are to be triggered when needed, and this too can be displayed on the board. For example, in the board in Figure 5-33, if the WIP limit on the first state crosses 4, it indicates that a planning meeting is needed.

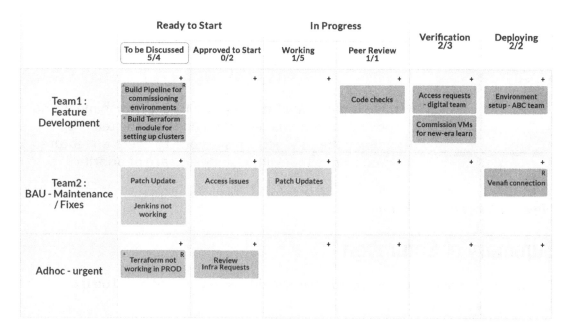

Figure 5-33. *Scrumban board with limits*

Best Practices in Scrumban

These are best practices for scrumban:

- Define and determine WIP limits to limit the backlog. This will help teams to stay focused and avoid missing any deadlines.

- The board should be easy to understand and stay relevant. Avoid having multiple swim lanes or transition states.

- Avoid multitasking and focus on completing work in progress rather than starting a new work item. Identify any unplanned tasks and risks and communicate them to meet the deadlines. See Figure 5-34.

Figure 5-34. *Did you know?*

Summary of Scrumban

Teams that are keen in adopting Scrumban should assess the need based on the following key factors:

- They tried Scrum with the team, but it was not successful due to frequent changes to stories.

- Priorities keep changing and are difficult to deliver as planned.

- The team needs to track enhancements along with the general product operations support.

- There is a strong need for making teams accountable for their deliveries and cultivating an agile mindset.

- The team is looking for a flexible model of operating workloads. The focus is to pull work without pushing work.

Thus, this methodology is good for projects that are struggling with agile but are not able to follow the principles and need some level of flexibility. The culture of "pulling" work is also an important practice as the team progresses. Through continuous practice, such teams become self-sufficient since they learn the art of managing and prioritizing work.

Summary

Let's look at the key differences between Scrum, Kanban, and scrumban. See Table 5-10.

Table 5-10. *Comparison of Agile Methods*

Description	Scrum	Kanban	Scrumban
Definition	An agile method for IT projects that focuses on delivering outcomes in frequent intervals	An agile method for IT projects that focuses on visualizing work by limiting work in progress	An agile method that leverages the best practices from Scrum and Kanban
Core objectives	• Cross-functional teams • Frequent deliverables (sprint based) • Prescriptive nature	• SRE teams • Frequent changes • Process improvement	• Deliver work in small intervals as well as limit work in progress • Build specialized teams
Key roles	• Scrum master • Product owner • Team	No predefined role, but the project manager will connect team members.	Scrum team + additional needed roles if needed
Basic construct	• Scrum team • Sprint board • Backlogs	• Kanban team • Kanban board	Scrumban/Kanban board
Key ceremonies	• Sprint planning • Daily standup • Sprint review • Retrospective	• WIP review	Daily Scrum
Key metrics	• Burndown chart • Velocity chart	• Lead time • Cycle time	• Lead time • Cycle time
Cadence	Fixed-length sprint	Continuous flow	Continuous flow with frequent releases

Having gone through the various agile methodologies available to infrastructure and DevOps teams, let's now understand how we can leverage these methodologies in infrastructure and cloud operations.

CHAPTER 6

Introduction to Agile Frameworks

In this chapter, we will discuss different delivery models that are defining agile ways of working and that are also introducing new roles into the system. The topics that will be covered in this chapter are as follows:

- Agile ITSM

- IT4IT

- Lean IT

- Scaled Agile Framework (SAFe®)

- Spotify

- Large Scaled Scrum (LeSS)

- Nexus

- Disciplined Agile Delivery (DAD)

- Site reliability engineering

Agile ITSM

As ITSM has evolved, there arose a need to complement rapid digitization and emerging needs. Organizations identified gaps that needed attention such as fragmented ITSM tools, limited standardization, etc., and looked at alternates to ITSM. While classic ITSM was well accepted by many organizations, there was a growing need for agility. Organizations looked for guidance to run their Service Delivery phase effectively in an agile way. This gave birth to *agile ITSM*, which borrowed some of the important

© Navin Sabharwal, Raminder Rathore, and Udita Agrawal 2022
N. Sabharwal et al., *Hands-On Guide to AgileOps*, https://doi.org/10.1007/978-1-4842-7505-4_6

principles of agile and constructed a methodology that stressed streamlining, optimization, and integrations. Organizations adopting agile principles found it easy to link up with various ITIL stages and use this new agile ITSM way of working.

Agile ITSM = Agile software development + ITSM

If agile talks about "working software," then ITIL stresses "focus on value." Hence, organizations are finding it easy to gel both agile and ITIL principles. As shown in Figure 6-1, an agile methodology like Scrum was tied to different phases in ITIL. While the product vision is mapped with the Service Strategy phase, the actual Scrum process starts with the Service Design phase where user stories requirements are recorded and prioritized in a backlog. The Service Transition phase has the sprints in a time-boxed schedule. The final phase is Service Operations, where the product is deployed through approved requests for change (RFCs).

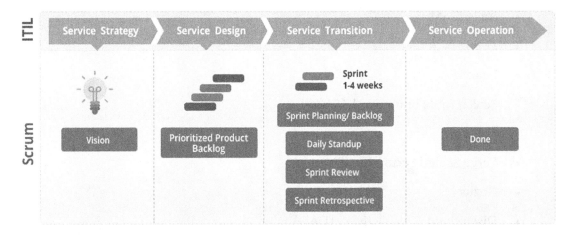

Figure 6-1. *ITIL and agile principles*

The only concern initially with this approach was that agile focused on iterations and ITIL executed in a sequential manner. Organizations adopting agile ITSM found a way out from this too. They motivated teams to work with a DevOps mindset that always targeted stability and agility. The infrastructure operations team is involved in the Service Design phase and provides all the necessary inputs that are needed for the warranty requirements. If ITSM revolved around stringent release and change management to control change, this agile ITSM was tackled by deciding on the amount and frequency of change control needed. This change control often is led by the product owner to manage the product as well as the sprint backlogs. In fact, it is the product owner who approves the CAB requests since the product owner manages the sprint backlog.

The agile ITSM method is a success since it ties the best practices of both ITIL and agile worlds, driven by a DevOps mindset. The associated roles in both methods also converged. For example, the roles of a product owner in the Scrum methodology and the service owner in ITIL were merged since the expectation from both roles was to be the voice of the customer.

IT4IT

IT4IT is a reference architecture that illustrates an operating model for managing IT. It is a powerful modern tool that helps organizations to manage their digital journey. This standard is being accepted and implemented by organizations of varied sizes with a key focus on driving interoperability, improving existing capabilities, and rationalizing applications. The standard also means to solve issues such as slow and manual activities linked with code management, packaging, deployment, and configuration management. (The IT4IT framework and its value streams come from `https://www.opengroup.org/it4it`, and IT4IT is a trademark of the Open Group.) The framework comprises four value streams that iteratively operate to deliver value and measures to improve, as shown in Figure 6-2.

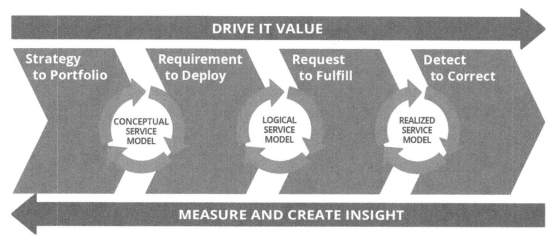

© The Open Group

Figure 6-2. *IT4IT value streams (reference: `https://www.opengroup.org/it4it`)*

- *Strategy to Portfolio (S2)*: Interconnects different functions that are involved in managing a portfolio of services delivered to fulfill an enterprise strategy. This value stream allows IT to contribute to enterprise strategy and planning. It also provides a holistic view on IT portfolio activities to understand the relationships between all the teams under the IT umbrella. It also comprises key functional and auxiliary components that drive the key activities.

- *Requirement to Deploy (R2D)*: Controls the quality, schedule, and cost of services regardless of delivery model. The idea behind this value stream is to accelerate sourcing and service delivery with best practices. Successful R2D is possible through a clear definition on scope, service blueprints, policies, and problem statements. Like S2P, R2D also has various functional components that process and deploy data objects.

- *Request to Fulfill (R2F)*: Emphasizes time to value, repeatability, and consistency for customers needing IT service support. It focuses on the relevance of deploying standard changes rather than delivering normal or custom changes. It helps organizations move toward a service broker model. It primarily focuses on system of record integrations between the functional components.

- *Detect to Correct (D2C)*: Increases efficiency, reduces cost and risk, and drives continuous improvements. This is achieved through automation, self-service, faster time to market, reducing MTTR, defining clear ownership, and improved management. A key goal of D2C is to manage IT efficiently by monitoring and automating key services, correlating, and managing incidents or events effectively and quickly. See Figure 6-3.

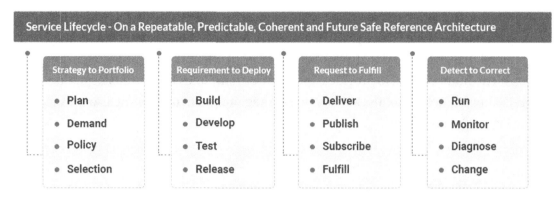

Figure 6-3. *IT4IT overview*

Each stream offers a list of key performance indicators (KPIs) that help in defining organizations' success toward its adoption, as shown in Table 6-1.

Table 6-1. *Value Stream and Its KPIs*

Value Stream	Key KPIs
S2P	• CapEx versus OpEx • Percent of software license consumption • Frequency of security assessments • Average cost/service or application
R2D	• Percent of actual versus planned executed tests • Percent of automated tests • Planned cost versus actual cost • Percent reduction in rework
R2F	• Number of completed service requests • Percent of WIP within SLAs • Percent of completed work within SLAs • Number of incidents for request fulfillment
D2C	• OLA versus SLA • Reduction in outages • Number of problems identified and removed • Percent of time invested on business-critical services

Various organizations adopt IT4IT at an enterprise scale using SAFe®, which helps them to increase release velocity. IT4IT describes the best tools architecture and related integrations that are needed to drive an effective implementation of SAFe®/agile and DevOps. The framework also provides open source templates for IT transformation programs, tool interoperability, and service management encompassing everything in IT. See Figure 6-4 and Table 6-2.

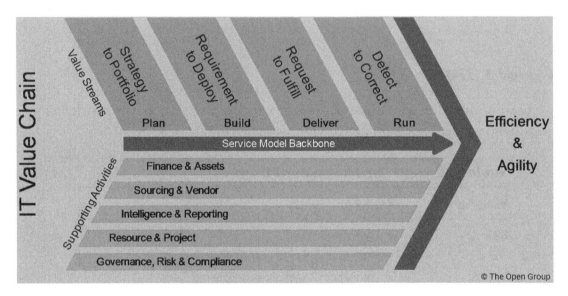

Figure 6-4. *IT4IT reference architecture (reference:* `https://www.opengroup.org/it4it`*)*

Table 6-2. *IT4IT Ways of Working*

Process Area	Traditional Way	Modern Way
S2P	Waterfall	Agile
R2D	Process heavy	Optimized
R2F	Manual	Automated
D2C	Siloed	Connected

IT4IT is a reference framework similar to ITIL; while ITIL focuses on managing IT, IT4IT focuses on IT service management (see Figure 6-5). In the infrastructure IT operations world, both have been used on a large scale, and enterprises have gotten the benefits of standardization using these processes and best practices.

Figure 6-5. *IT4IT versus ITIL*

Lean IT

Lean is an integrated system of principles, practices, and techniques for operational excellence based on empowering the front line and driving a relentless pursuit of perfect customer value creation. The lean IT framework extends the principles of lean services. It promises to identify and remove waste so that customer service is improved. There has been significant growth in the demand for IT services, and this has brought in variability in service offerings. The cost of expertise and environment setup has also grown. With an increase in complexity and demand, there is a need to look at improving the flow and eliminating waste. See Figure 6-6.

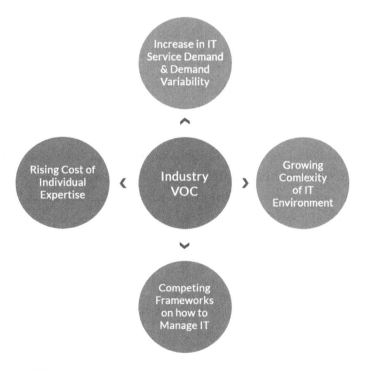

Figure 6-6. *Lean IT overview*

What is *not* lean IT?

- It is not just process redesigning.

- It is not limited to just tools and techniques.

- It is not a one-time improvement program.

- It is not a new flavor of Six Sigma.

But what is a waste in IT? There could be various types of wastes that can be remembered as the abbreviation DOWNTIME.

- *Defects*: Issues are found in production due to insufficient testing. Defects are bugs, errors, or mistakes that exist in software. Leaked defects in production are costly and need rework.

- *Over production*: In the current era, the customer prioritizes requirements and expects them to be delivered frequently and in shorter cycles. Releasing requirements that have low value or with a lower priority in comparison to higher-priority requirements is not what the customer demands. This is where prioritized backlogs are being used for requirements.

- *Waiting*: This is related to the idle time between steps in the process and workflow among different team transitions on a task.

- *Non-value-added processing*: Any process or step in a workflow that is not adding value is a waste. Excessive documentation in the current era of agile is not needed.

- *Transportation*: There is a knowledge loss when it is transitioned or transferred to other people within or outside the team. The requirements when shared from one person to another person sometimes change due to a difference in understanding. This leads to misunderstood requirements.

- *Inventory*: There is a saying, "Stop starting and start completing." This is relevant for the tasks when picked up should be completed before picking up the new task as customers demand value to be delivered. Some examples of Inventory are unutilized resources, like large number of repositories or branches that are not required and are not being used.

- *Motion*: This points to the list of manual and mundane repetitive activities that involve a lot of time that otherwise could be spent on thinking of and creating new services or improving existing services.

- *Employee knowledge*: People's skillsets are not rightly aligned with the work. The right practices need to be aligned so that employee knowledge is being used at the right place.

Now that we have seen the categories of waste, let's understand the five core principles of lean IT.

- *Value*: The value needs to be defined from a customer's perspective. The focus is on the services delivered.

- *Map the value stream*: The value stream maps all the steps, efforts, inputs, and outputs that are value-added or non-value-added.

- *Flow*: The services and information flow from end to end through the process. The flow should be defined in such a way as to have a smooth delivery of services.

- *Pull*: Work and deliver customer needs when they are asked and required.

- *Seek perfection*: This is the complete elimination of waste to provide value to a customer through all the tasks. This is possible through continuous improvements and continuous feedback. See Figure 6-7.

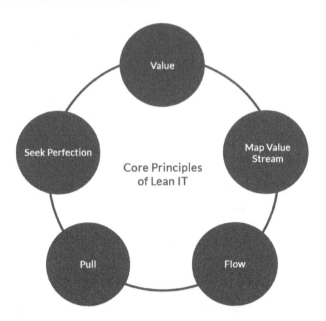

Figure 6-7. *Lean IT core principles*

The core principles of lean IT are observed in the SAFe® agile method covered in the next section. While teams work in agile mode, they target flexibility, adaptability, and improving customer satisfaction. To speed up deliveries, it is important to analyze the workflow and identify areas that are consuming time and hampering the delivery schedule. Hence, both agile and lean help teams to visualize work, to continuously learn and collaborate, and to measure project progress across each iteration. Lean also offers an important principle called *value stream processing* that helps to identify the waste to make the process more efficient. This is done through a value stream assessment process, which is used to assess the strengths and weaknesses of an enterprise's value stream.

The steps in the value stream assessment process are as follows:

1. Select a product/service/flow.

2. Involve the stakeholders.

3. Understand the voice of the customer.

4. Develop the current state value stream map.

5. Identify waste.

6. Develop the future-state value stream map.

7. Determine the benefits.

8. Develop the implementation plan.

9. Implement the future-state VSM.

10. Analyze and fine-tune the future-state VSM.

Interestingly, value stream mapping is also leveraged as a measure to assess an organization's maturity on DevOps. Various templates are available that help teams to document the current state that focuses on the quality of work delivered, the percentage of rework done, the lead and cycle time on delivering working software, etc. See Figure 6-8.

Figure 6-8. *Ingredients for successful product development*

The key ingredients for successful product development depend on how lean, agile, and DevOps have been adopted and practiced by the team. These three portions complement each other and define new ways of working. The core foundation is the customer need, or the value that needs to be delivered within an optimized cost model.

While lean focuses on building the right things in an optimized way, agile focuses on building the thing right. The shift from traditional ways to modern ways is a growing expectation and cannot be put aside anymore. Process-heavy, manual activities are to be optimized and automated. Siloed teams need to connect and collaborate continuously. Lean IT is an approach to align IT with the business. It is a goal-oriented framework that focuses on team empowerment. When complemented with agile and DevOps, it does wonders for organizations. See Figure 6-9.

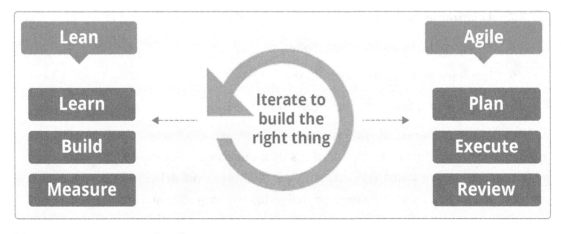

Figure 6-9. *Lean and agile*

Scaled Agile Framework® (SAFe®)

The Scaled Agile Framework® (SAFe®) is the leading framework for organizations seeking to embrace Business Agility and thrive in the post-digital economy. SAFe® was introduced in 2011 by Dean Leffingwell, et. al. Recognizing the challenges of time to market and quality among large scale solution providers, the authors sought to bring alignment, collaboration, and transparency to even the most complicated business and technology organizations. The framework is a series of processes and tools derived from years of observing patterns across enterprises, rooted in a Lean-Agile mindset, core values, and ten immutable underlying Lean-Agile principles; these are –

- #1 Take an economic view

- #2 Apply systems thinking

- #3 Assume variability; preserve options

- #4 Build incrementally with fast integrated learning cycles

- #5 Base milestones on objective evaluation of working systems

- #6 Visualize and limit Work-In-Progress, reduce batch sizes, and manage queue lengths

- #7 Apply cadence, synchronize with cross domain planning

- #8 Unlock the intrinsic motivation of knowledge workers

- #9 Decentralize decision-making

- #10 Organize around value

SAFe® is highly configurable to address each organization's intent and purpose. It offers different configurations (Essential, Large Solution, Portfolio and Full) that can easily be adopted by any organization. One key element that is common amongst all these configurations is the concept of the Agile Release Train (ART). An ART delivers a value stream to the organization; it is comprised of 5-12 Agile teams (with ~50-125 cross functional experts across different departments) that work together in iterations called Program Increments (PIs). All the features which are planned for the PI are delivered through the train. If a feature is not a part of the planned PI, then it will not get started till the next increment begins. Also, an ART maps with the sprint cycles. Since teams within the ART should be aligned they need to follow the same start and end dates for their sprints. Every ART has a role called the Release Train Engineer (RTEs- functions like a Scrum Master); who facilitates the release cycle.

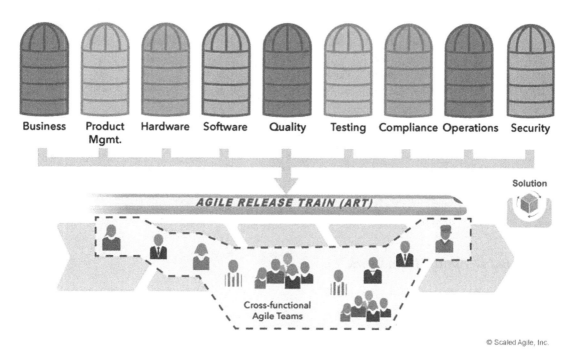

Figure 6-10. *ART in SAFe®*

Spotify

Spotify is one of the most popular audio streaming services in the world. The Spotify model is all about the company's approach for enhancing team agility. The model was first introduced in 2012. The model focuses on people, culture, and an autonomous approach on scaling agile. It is an example of how multiple teams are organized in a product development organization by adopting a change in culture and how we collaborate and network.

The model differs from others as it focuses on organizing around work and restructuring the organization on the basis of business to enhance agility rather than following specific set of practices such as daily standups, planning meetings, etc.

The teams in the Spotify model decide which framework to adopt, be it Kanban, Scrum, scrumban, etc. The way the team is structured is very different than the traditional agile frameworks. Let's understand the basic terms used in this framework. See Figure 6-11.

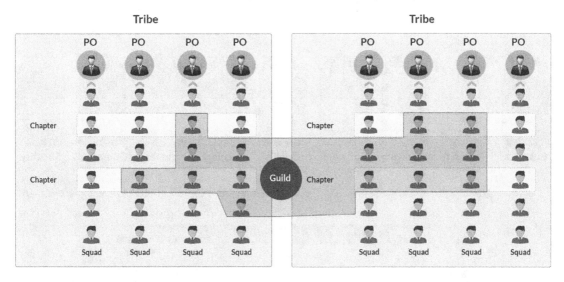

Figure 6-11. *Spotify framework*

Squad: Squad teams are cross-functional teams with six to ten members. The team has a mission and are supported by an agile coach and product owner.

Tribe: At times, certain people need to work across squads on features, so they form a tribe. A tribe consists of a large number of people unlike squads. Each tribe has a tribe leader who aligns, coordinates among squads, and fosters collaboration.

Chapter: Chapters are standards and best practices that enable the team to do their work. Typically, a chapter has a leader who is mostly a senior technical lead or an architect. Chapters are formed within a tribe.

Guild: A guild is a forum where people join out of interest about a specific topic. This is voluntary and spans tribes unlike chapters. There is no specific leader for a guild, but anyone can volunteer to coordinate the activities of a guild and bring everyone together.

Trio: Trio is a combination of a tribe lead, product lead, and design lead. Trio is part of each tribe and ensures alignment in a tribe on the three core areas of a product.

Alliance: A trio sometimes works together toward a bigger common goal of the organization where multiple tribes need to work together.

Let's assume that the enterprise Alpha needs to transform into a Spotify model. As evident in Figure 6-12, organizations will have various product teams, and each will have squads and chapters running either vertically or horizontally.

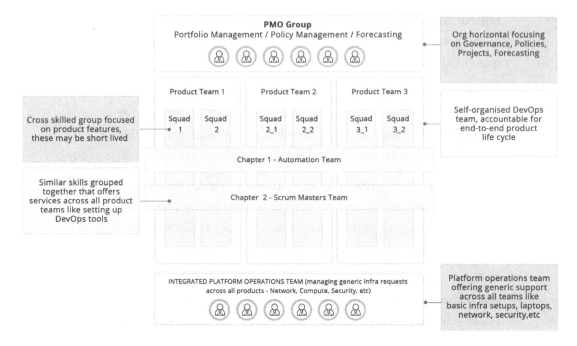

Figure 6-12. *Squad-chapter agile model*

Each product team can have multiple squad teams based on requirements, and as soon as they complete a product feature, they can be regrouped to plan for another product feature. Each squad is a dedicated team that knows what is to be developed and plans accordingly. Chapters, on other hand, focus on how things can be delivered. For example, these can be thought of as communities of practice like Scrum masters. These Scrum masters get aligned with product teams for guiding and implementing agile practices, and when the team is self-sufficient, they return to the community and get aligned with another product team. These squads and chapters can adopt their own agile methodology that suits them best. Each product team can have multiple squads, and they work together to ensure that the product is delivered from end to end leveraging the available DevOps tooling. Apart from these squads and chapters, of course there are other important functions such as PMO, security, and platform operations that horizontally provide support for everyone across the organization.

Such a model seems to be difficult to implement initially, but a phased plan helps enterprises achieve this goal smoothly over a defined time. It is important to note that the new structure demands new roles, new tools, and training needs, and this should be the prerequisite before jumping to this new model. The goal is to ensure that agility is the core principle for every team, and that can be achieved with the right process mining, goal setting, new role definitions, and introduction to new technology to save time and effort.

This framework also introduces a few new role definitions, as shown in Table 6-3.

Table 6-3. *Roles in Spotify*

New Role	Portfolio Level
Squad lead	• Orchestrates work and builds a collaborative team • Mentors the team and provides feedback for improvements • Embraces the culture of accountability • Collaborates with chapter leads
Chapter lead	• Performs as a line manager • Provides specialized support across different squads • Tracks and delivers high-quality services
SRE	• Cross-skilled engineers, part of chapters • Specialized in emerging technologies like IaC, DevOps, the cloud, etc.

The Spotify model is a well-tested framework for infrastructure operations teams that can scale in sprints and redefine their operations organization structure. To transition our example company Alpha into a Spotify working organization, the following items need to be addressed first:

- Coach all team members on agile concepts. Existing operations teams with the culture of "push" need to be mentored on "pulling work" and getting accountable.

- Encourage them to ask questions and embrace the upcoming change. Teams need to be encouraged to move on the new path of agility that will benefit them.

- Identify tools that are needed in the new ecosystem. As teams learn the agile methods, they also need to learn new tools that will make them effective. They should be trained on how to create and refer to dashboards, view team progress, and understand the basics of "work in progress," as well as how their contribution will lead to the success of the engagement.

- Form a new organization structure that comprises squads, chapters, guilds, and tribes. This structure should also be evangelized with the teams so that they understand the purpose of each team.

- Select the agile methodology that will be practiced by squads. The methodology should consider the maturity of the teams in understanding the methods like Scrum, Kanban, scrumban, etc., and their implementation. Agile adoption can be successful only when squads practice them regularly.

- Identity new roles to be introduced and map them with existing roles; otherwise, plan to hire. As the existing operations team gets trained, the team should be notified that the new structure will bring in new roles and responsibilities. They should be given an opportunity to volunteer for these new roles.

- Define the new operational organization structure that is mapped with new roles, tagged with team members. Collaborate with organization change management to broadcast this new change. Plan and run workshops to let teams know about the new change, which will avoid chaos within the teams. Alternatively, pilot and expand the structure. The new operations structure can be rolled out in a staggered manner instead of a big bang. This decision should be made by the executives based on their in-depth understanding of the ecosystem.

Let's assume Alpha is preparing for this new journey; the prerequisites are being taken care of, and now we need to draft an outline for the new model.

- New roles = product owner, squad lead, chapter lead, SREs, cloud engineers, and architects. You can identify existing roles that can be scaled to these new roles; for example, tower leads can be groomed to be squad leads.

- Horizontal teams = chapters, guilds. These service groups run through all the squads, and the members keep moving between different squads. Existing teams that run governance, compliance, etc., can be scaled to these new roles.

- Vertical teams = tribes, squads. These teams can be visualized as product teams that have pizza-sized teams scattered across different regions and working for different features.

For Alpha, we will plan for two tribes. The first tribe will fulfill requests for on-premises infrastructure, and the second one will fulfill cloud requests. We will call them on-premise tribe and cloud transformation.

Let's understand the organization structure, as shown in Figure 6-13.

- The on-premise tribe will support on-premises environments, and the cloud transformation tribe will support cloud environments.

- Team members will be grouped into squads, where each squad will have SREs who are cross-skilled experts on Unix, Wintel, messaging, backup, VMware, network, automation, etc.

- Each tribe will have three squads. The squads in a tribe target a defined set of workloads.

- A generic squad will be working on automation use cases.

- The innovate squad will work toward new integration and pilots.

- A global squad will address operational tasks across all regions.

- The squads will be led by mentors or leads who will empower teams on this new organization structure and way of working. The leads will also decide on the agile methodology that they will practice.

- Each squad will have its own product owner who will be working with the agile team.

- The DC generic/cloud generic team will follow Scrum to address development stories and tasks on automation threads.

- The DC innovate/cloud innovate team will follow the scrumban method to address stories and tasks for both development and operations for pilot rollouts and continuous research and development.

- The DC global/cloud global team will follow the Kanban method wherein operational user stories and tasks will be tracked and resolved.

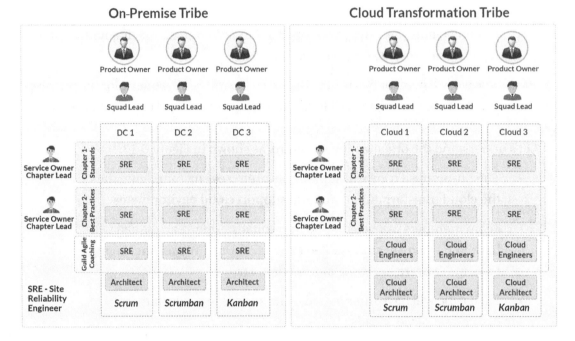

Figure 6-13. *Spotify model for InfraOps*

There will also be two chapters and guilds that function as horizontal services.

- Standards comprised of architects that define patterns, nomenclature, governing rules, etc.

- Best practices that serve as a community of practice across all the squads, sharing effective methods and tools needed to run an efficient pipeline or operation.

- Each chapter will be coordinated and managed by a service owner or chapter lead.

- The standards and best practices chapters both will have members from all the squads in that particular tribe. In our example, some members from all squads of the on-premise tribe will be part of the standards and best-practice chapters. Similarly, this will be applicable for the other tribe.

- In our example, a guild is specifically for agile coaching. This guild will have members from both tribes.

These were just examples; there can be more tribes such as for risks and compliance, release and automation, service desk, etc., which in turn will have its squads, chapters, and guilds.

The success of the Spotify model can be achieved by having the right culture mindset, giving autonomy to the teams, choosing the framework that best suits the team, adopting tools that are beneficial to them, encouraging teams to participate in guilds, building trust, motivating and appreciating people, and learning from mistakes.

LeSS

LeSS was introduced in 2005 by Bas Vodde and Craig Larman. The LeSS framework expands one team Scrum to multiple teams by scaling. (The references have been taken from https://less.works/less/framework.) LeSS applies Scrum principles, processes, and elements in a large team context where multiple teams work on a single product. All Scrum teams follow the same sprint, use the same product backlog, and have same one product owner.

Customer requirements in LeSS are categorized into requirement areas. Every product backlog item is part of only one requirement area. The requirements in a particular area are grouped together. This forms an area product backlog that is a subset of the product backlog. Items in the area product backlog are smaller when compared with the product backlog as those are broken down to be completed in one sprint. The product backlog items from the area product backlog get picked up by multiple teams working on that backlog. This is a different approach when compared to other scaled frameworks.

There are other LeSS frameworks such as Basic LeSS, which has two to eight teams, and LeSS Huge, which has more than eight teams. See Figure 6-14.

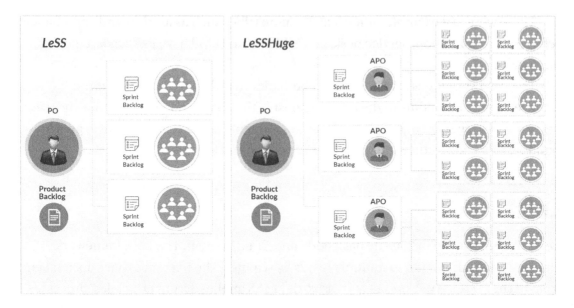

Figure 6-14. *LeSS overview*

LeSS has guides and experiments that have been carried out by people who introduced LeSS based on implementing scaled agile in multiple organizations.

In addition to the Scrum roles of product owner, Scrum master, and development team, LeSS has an additional role of a manager.

A manager in LeSS provides autonomy to the team to experiment and assists the team in removing barriers and improving continuously.

The area product owner (APO) key role in the LeSS Huge framework assists and coordinates with the product owner (PO) and bridges any gaps between the business and the technical teams. The roles and responsibilities of APO are like a PO. The final decision-making on a requirement and its prioritization in the product backlog lie with the PO rather than the APO, even though both work together. The APO also helps the PO from being overloaded. The APO focuses on customer-focused product features and works with the product owner on them. The area product backlog is managed by the APO, which in turn is used by multiple teams within an area. Also, the APO leads all these teams that are part of that area. See Figure 6-15.

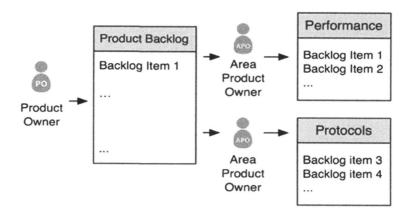

Figure 6-15. *Product owner and area product owner*
(reference: https://less.works/less/less-huge/area-product-owner)

In addition to the regular Scrum ceremonies, there is an additional product backlog refinement meeting that focuses on product backlog refinement considering priority, estimation, breakdown of bigger stories, identification of risks, and dependencies.

An Example

Let's consider our earlier enterprise Alpha that needs to be transitioned from a traditional approach to a LeSS Huge framework. This enterprise has both the on-premises and cloud environments, and we need to create a new structure made up of teams that will work on automation through IaC. The following roles and team structures are needed to roll out the LeSS framework:

- New roles = product owner who will manage groups that are led by the area product owners. Each squad will be led by a squad lead or a Scrum master, and each squad will have architects and cross-skilled engineers called SREs that manage both type of environments.

- Vertical structure = groups. These teams are further made up of squads that have a defined purpose. Moreover, each squad can choose an agile method that best suits their working culture. See Figure 6-16.

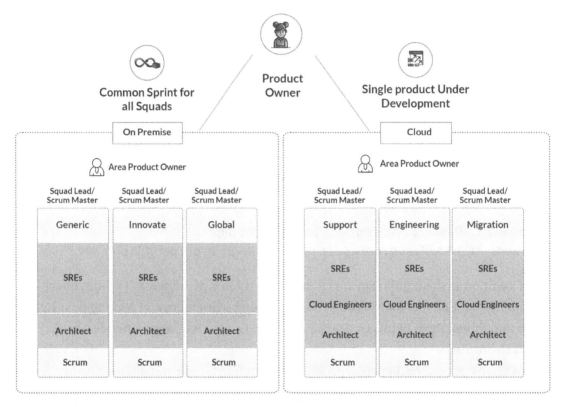

Figure 6-16. *LeSS structure*

To implement LeSS, we need to form two groups of squads. The on-premise group of squads will be called Generic, Innovate, and Global, each having a Scrum master, SREs, and an infrastructure architect. The new infrastructure squads will have cross-skilled people with Unix, Windows, VMware, AppOps, DBA, and networking skills. Similarly, the cloud group will have three more squads that work together supporting cloud-related tasks such as supporting existing teams, migrating on-premises applications to the cloud, and engineering on extensions and integrations. The on-premises and cloud groups will have their own area product owner (APO). This APO will work very closely with teams to share product requirements. There will be only one product owner (PO) that will manage this service. The PO here is responsible for all the infrastructure support and automation activities, be it on premise or on the cloud. So, in this example there are two groups that continue supporting business-as-usual work activities along with the development of automation pipelines for migrating applications to the cloud. A single product backlog will be managed and prioritized by this product owner. All the squads will follow the same sprints and work toward a common business goal, which is to maximize infrastructure automation. Thus, LeSS focuses on building an end-to-end product by multiple teams working together on the same product following the same sprints, but working in in different groups, though.

Nexus

The Nexus framework was introduced in 2015 by Ken Schwaber who is a co-creator of Scrum framework available at Scrum.org (`https://www.scrum.org/resources/scaling-scrum`). Nexus is based on the Scrum framework and uses an iterative and incremental product delivery approach. It is useful for organizations where multiple teams work on the same product and integrate as a larger team.

It works well with three to nine teams where each team is again a small team of eight to ten people, all working together on the same product. All teams work toward a common goal. See Figure 6-17.

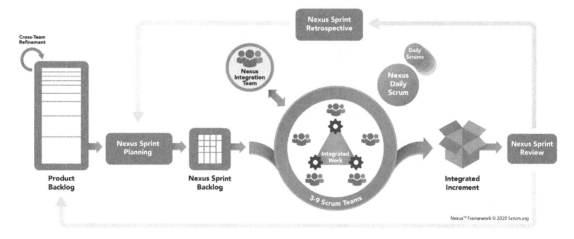

Figure 6-17. *Nexus framework (reference: `https://www.scrum.org/resources/scaling-scrum`)*

It differs from Scrum as it does not have a product owner for each team; instead, there is one product owner for all teams. There is one common product backlog that is managed by the product owner, and Scrum teams pull work from it. In addition to the regular roles of Scrum like Scrum master, product owner, and developers, Nexus has a new accountability role, which is the Nexus integration team.

The Nexus integration team ensures every sprint is an integrated product from all the teams that is ready and delivered. Scrum teams integrate the code, but focus and accountability lie with the integration team for a sprint-integrated product. The integration team has a product owner, Scrum master, and required integration team members who will resolve technical issues when needed. The integration team is also accountable for coaching and mentoring the Scrum teams to follow and learn the practices and tools to implement and develop the product with quality. So, the key difference in this model is that rather than integration happening through an ART, there is a separate team whose job is to integrate.

Events are similar to in Scrum; they include the Nexus planning meeting, Nexus daily Scrum, Nexus sprint review, Nexus sprint retrospective, and cross-team refinement.

Cross-team refinement is done for the product backlog to help identify the dependencies among the teams and also plans which Scrum teams will deliver which items from the product backlog.

An Example

In the traditional model, code integration is a big challenge when multiple code bases are to be integrated. And during integration, many hidden defects are identified. The integration team that works on code integration and resolves code merger issues helps a lot in such scenarios. See Figure 6-18.

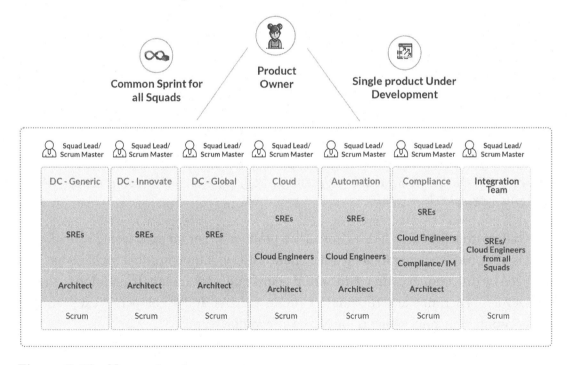

Figure 6-18. *Nexus structure*

Let's transform our imaginary traditional company Alpha into the Nexus framework. The following will be the new elements that will get introduced into the system:

- New roles = product owner, squad lead/Scrum master, SREs, architects, and cloud engineers.

- Vertical structures = squads. There could be a number of squads that work together to deliver an enterprise theme or epic, for example, delivering a self-service catalog.

Teams will be transformed into six squads or teams, having a Scrum master, SREs, cloud engineers, and architect. There will be three DC squads called Generic, Innovate, and Global. These DC squads will have cross-skilled people with UNIX, VMware, network, Windows, DBA, and AppOps skills. The cloud squad will manage and deliver components and services on the cloud. The other two squads will be for automation and compliance, with automation, DevOps, cloud, IM, and compliance management skills separate from infrastructure. All the squads will have one common product owner since there is one product that needs to be managed and developed. A single product backlog will be managed and prioritized by the product owner. Unlike the other scaled agile team structure, Nexus has an additional integration team that will have team members from the DC, cloud, automation, and compliance squads. They work on integration issues for the integrated sprint deliverable from all squads. All the squads will follow the same sprints and work toward a common business goal.

Thus, for teams where Scrum is fully implemented and there is one product to be developed, the Nexus model is the best to adopt.

Disciplined Agile Delivery (DAD)

The DAD framework was introduced in 2009 by IBM under the guidance of Scott Ambler and Mark Lines. It is also similar to SAFe® when adopting the principles of lean and agile. It is a process-driven framework that focuses on interaction between people and within the organization. See Figure 6-19.

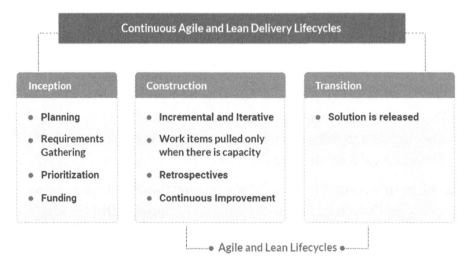

Figure 6-19. *Disciplined agile delivery framework*

Its delivery cycle consists of three distinct phases:

Inception: In the Inception phase, the team is formed, the project vision is formed and aligned with the organization vision, the scope is identified, the architecture and technical strategy along with the testing strategy are formed, the initial plan and release gets decided, the funding is secured, and the risks are identified.

Construction: This is all about developing a consumable solution, creating an architecture, improving quality, addressing stakeholder requirements, and moving closer to release and delivering value.

Transition: This is the phase where team ensures the solution is ready for deployment and performs the deployment.

There are primary and secondary team roles. The primary roles are the team lead, product owner, architecture owners, team members, and stakeholders, whereas the secondary roles are the testers, technical experts, etc., which interact with the team and the environment for developing a workable solution. The ceremonies are also similar to the Scrum framework.

There are two scaling angles for DAD.

Tactical agility at scale: This address scaling for team factors such as size, geography, complexity of project, etc., through the application of processes and standards.

Strategic agility at scale: This address scaling for different areas of the organization through the agile and lean strategies.

Thus, the organization can decide which DAD scaling method is required as per applicability.

Table 6-4 highlights some key differences of some of the frameworks mentioned so far.

Table 6-4. *Quick differences on some of the Agile Frameworks*

Description	LeSS	Spotify	Nexus
Definition	An agile Scrum framework for scaling Scrum to multiple teams. It provides two variants:LeSS, up to eight member teams, andLeSS HUGE, up to a few thousand people in one product.	A people-driven, autonomous approach for scaling agile that emphasizes the importance of culture and network.	An agile Scrum framework where multiple teams work on a single product portfolio and create an integrated increment.
Core objectives	1. Lean thinking 2. Systems thinking 3. Whole-product focus 4. Customer centric 5. Continuous improvement	1. Self-management 2. Flexibility by focusing on organizing work 3. Focus on culture	1. Empiricism and self-management 2. Organizing around value 3. Ensures transparency 4. Focus on continuous integration and continuous improvement

(continued)

Table 6-4. (*continued*)

Description	LeSS	Spotify	Nexus
Key roles	1. Product owner 2. Scrum master 3. Team 4. Area product owner	1. Squads (6–7 members) 2. Tribes (40–150 members) 3. Chapters (specialists from within same tribe) 4. Guilds (communities of interest) 5. Trio (tribe lead, product lead, design lead) 6. Chief architect	1. Product owner (one for all) 2. Scrum master 3. Team 4. Nexus integration team
Basic construct	1. One team Scrum 2. One DoD for all teams 3. One sprint	1. Tribe engineering model 2. Guilds and chapters	1. One sprint for all teams 2. Teams (three to nine Scrum teams) 3. Nexus integration team for integrating increments of each team 4. One product owner for all teams
Key ceremonies	1. Sprint planning (part 1 and 2) 2. Daily Scrum 3. Sprint review 4. Product backlog refinement (PBR) 5. Overall retrospective	1. Squads adopt either Scrum or Kanban and follow the ceremonies 2. Retrospectives	1. Nexus sprint planning 2. Nexus sprint review 3. Nexus sprint retrospective 4. Refinement 5. Nexus daily Scrum

(*continued*)

Table 6-4. (*continued*)

Description	LeSS	Spotify	Nexus
Key metrics	1. Burndown chart 2. Velocity chart	1. Lead time 2. Cycle time 3. Velocity chart	1. Nexus sprint goal (sum of all work and sprint goals) 2. Nexus integrated increment (current sum of all integrated work that has been completed)
Cadence	Fixed-length sprint	Weeks	2 to 4 weeks

Site Reliability Engineering

SRE is an application-first, reliability-first approach to IT operations and a set of best practices including metrics focused on availability and errors. The SRE concept originated in the early 2000s at Google to provide support to complex and global infrastructure at Google. The term was coined by Treynor Sloss, Google's VP of engineering.

As the name suggests, the primary focus of SRE is system reliability. The SRE team also focuses on developing health monitoring, deployment automation, and other such tasks that enhance the reliability of the overall system.

SRE Guiding Principles

Now let's look at the seven key SRE principles that describe processes needed to implement DevOps principles.

> *Embrace risk*: We all acknowledge the fact that services cannot be 100 percent reliable. Teams make continuous efforts to improve and maintain the reliability score, because it impacts the customer satisfaction. Of course, improving reliability demands investments. When risks are embraced, we get to know when such investments are unnecessary and when they are really needed. Overspending on reliability may decrease development velocity,

and organizations will not favor this. The principle of embracing risk has a cultural component too (the key toward DevOps adoption), wherein teams should feel secure when they are taking risks to accelerate development. This is possible by determining the following factors that the teams can refer to always:

- Risk of not implementing an improvement request. Analyze the ripple effect when a change request is not implemented; this will lead to a major impact that may result in making a customer unhappy.

- Acceptance level of reliability for customers. Look at the usage patterns, collect feedback, and define the SLO and SLI (described in the next principle) values to gain team confidence.

- Cost for implementing a change that may increase reliability. Study the associated costs that are needed for improving services that will have a positive impact on the business.

- Estimate the costs associated with the risks and share it with the teams so that they understand the impact and make wise decisions.

- *Define service level objectives (SLOs)*: Every organization signs a legal agreement with their customers that comprises of a set of service level agreements (SLAs). These SLAs are commitments with the customer, ensuring that the service will be available for their consumption. For example, servers will be available 99.9 percent of the time. To ensure that these SLAs are not breached, companies map these SLAs into internal goals calling them SLOs, and these are further translated into service level indicators (SLIs). While an SLO helps teams to manage risks and budget for any errors, an SLI notifies teams for an action to be taken before a service causes pain to their customers. See Table 6-5.

Table 6-5. *Comparison of Service Levels*

Service Level Indicator (SLI)	Service Level Objective (SLO)	Service Level Agreement (SLA)
The actual performance that comprises key measures like the following: • Response time including wait time • Error rate in requests per second • Request rate in requests per second • Utilization percentage	Define goals for the team that must meet the SLA. A few targets can be as follows: • Defining lower and upper bounds for SLIs • Defining a target wherein SLI needs to be less than this target	An external-facing agreement shared with the customer that lists the commitments that the teams agree to

It is important that teams build effective SLOs and SLIs based on the customer's pain point, and they should revise (aligned with the DevOps principle of continuous feedback) these values as services mature.

- *Minimize toil*: Toil refers to the amount of redundant work that a team does frequently. In SRE, removing toil is another important principle that helps drive accelerated development and operations. This is possible through automation and optimization techniques. Teams can eliminate toil by observing the list of tasks that are time-consuming and recurring. By creating effective automation with guidelines and templates, one can reduce toil drastically, thus allowing teams to focus on other areas that need attention. Removing toil should be done in sprints (aligned with the DevOps principle of continuous improvement) so that teams get to monitor the benefits.

- *Monitoring*: There is a lot of meaningful data that is produced by the systems, and not all that data needs teams' attention. There are monitoring tools available to track, extract, and consolidate this data into useful metrics that help teams to derive decisions or take action to resolve issues. For an SRE, it is important that the following metrics (aligned with DevOps principle of continuous improvements) are tracked, which in turn are needed to measure SLIs.

- *Error rate*: Requests to service failure

- *Latency*: Time to respond

- *Traffic*: Amount of service load

- *Saturation*: Up to what duration the resources will last

- *Automation*: Development velocity can increase when automation tools are leveraged (which helps in aligning with the DevOps principle of continuous integration, continuous testing, and continuous deployment). Teams need to look at the processes in their product lifecycle that need to be automated and optimized. This demands investment in new tools and introducing practices like shift-left testing, automated deployment patterns, etc. Automation helps teams to reduce toil and increase team velocity. SREs should be encouraged to identify and implement automation solutions across different areas that will help them improve on turnaround time. For example, playbooks or runbooks are documents that list and describe diagnostic and remediation procedures so that everyone in the team is aware of what needs to be done when a situation presents. This results in lower mean time to resolve and standardization in action across various resources and teams. It is important that the playbooks are maintained and updated based on changes in infrastructure and application landscape and versions. Modern digital organizations have now moved to executable playbooks that are configured as playbooks in runbook automation or configuration management tools such as Operations Orchestrator, Ansible, Puppet, and Chef. A new breed of AI-driven intelligent automation tools like DRYiCE iAutomate provide capabilities that leverage NLP and AI technologies to further enhance the runbook automation capabilities to rapidly deploy the right runbooks in the environment and help in the automatic maintenance of the runbooks on an ongoing basis.

- *Release engineering*: As products and services are released frequently, managing releases becomes a tedious task. Irrespective of the number of releases, SREs need to ensure that the releases are consistently deployed (aligns with the DevOps principle of continuous deployment) through an optimized process workflow that leverages automated tools as well. For faster deployments, it is important to agree on and practice guidelines across different release types. This is possible when teams use the same set of standards, policies, and protocols for releasing their services. As releases grow in number, SREs should monitor the release statistics and analyze the release strategy in case it needs to be changed. For example, canary releases make rollouts safer and faster. With canary releases, the new features are introduced to a small set of users. This results in feedback on performance and on the user experience of the application, and once the release is successful, the new features are released to all users. This method de-risks the releases as all users are not simultaneously impacted. Canary releases cut the mean time to detect (MTTD) an issue by quickly surfacing issues in applications when they are used by real users (a subset of the total population of users).

- *Simplicity*: Reliability often is complemented with simplicity. Any service that is simple to deploy, monitor, repair, and improve is a reliable candidate. Simple systems are easy to manage and update. SREs can model systems to analyze areas of complexity and find ways to simplify it. Teams should be encouraged to collaborate (aligns with the DevOps principle of collaboration) and design simple systems and also should be made aware that complex systems demand huge investments, such as removing nodes and connections that are not needed.

In addition to these seven principles, there are other principles too that are important for SREs to practice.

- *Treat operations as a software problem*: This aspect aligns fairly well with the "no more silos" principle in DevOps, which aims to bring together infrastructure and applications. When SRE was first introduced, not many organizations would have software-defined infrastructure and infrastructure as code; however, today this principle can be adopted as technology has evolved to support infrastructure changes as software changes.

- *Find error budgets*: This is another important principle in SRE operations, and this aspect aligns fairly well with the "metrics" principle in DevOps where the aim is to capture the metrics to improve. The goal of the SRE is to deliver services that are well within the error budget; this serves as a guiding metric for the SREs to determine both the architectural and operations aspects of services. The SREs balance the agility to deliver the features fast without compromising availability. The error budget is used to keep a check on releases and velocity, which means that in case there is no budget for errors, the SRE team will put a stop to releases that can impact availability further. SREs need to discuss the error budgets with the product management team and define availability targets for a service. They also need to discuss additional costs such as adding more fault tolerance (if need arises) or things like reducing frequencies or testing times.

Interestingly, a system's acceptable risk dictates the SLOs, and the SLOs in turn drive the error budgets. For example, if a service incurs too much downtime, then one should reduce risk to remain within SLOs. Based on the product features, availability, and usage, one should define the right SLOs. For example, a 99.9 percent SLO indicates that the system should be available for 99.9 percent of the time. So, in a month, only 0.1 percent downtime is allowed, and if we calculate this in minutes, it comes out to be as follows:

= [0.001] * [30 days] * [24 hours] * [60 mins]

=43.2 minutes of downtime allowed in a month.

So, if the system goes down for more than 43.2 minutes, then this will breach the commitments. Hence, it is important to understand the product offerings and the service availability levels, and this will help in calculating the error budgets. Let's explore further with an example where availability and SLOs are defined, and we need to find the error budget.

a.   System availability = 90%

b.   SLO = 80%

c.   So, the Error budget = Availability – SLO; which when calculated with values from (a) and (b) .i.e. 90% - 80%; results to 10%. Thus, the error budget value is 10%.

d.   This when translated into months results into 72 hours in a month.

This means that even if the product is down for up to three days in a month, it will not breach the SLAs.

- *Reduce the cost of failure*: This aspect corresponds to the two guiding principles in DevOps that are "gradual changes" and "failures are normal." The SRE team focuses on resolving the problems early in the cycle of development so that the failures do not impact production systems. There are various processes and practices that the SRE team uses to achieve this end objective. Involvement of SREs in the design and architecture stages helps to proactively plan for high availability and in the case of a failure restore quickly and thus reduce the cost of failure.

- *Roll back early, roll back often*: When errors are found or suspected, the first thing the team does is to roll back to the previous version and then continue to explore the problem. Thus, the first step is to recover the system and then focus on exploring the problem and undertaking problem management. This results in a higher availability of systems and services and a lower mean time to resolve. See Figure 6-20.

DID YOU KNOW?

MTTD vs MTTF vs MTBF vs MTTR ?

MTTD - Mean Time To Detect, average amount of time it takes to discover an issue.
MTTF - Mean Time To Fail, average amount of time a defective system can continue running before it fails.
MTBF - Mean Time Between Failures, a metric to measure the ability of a system to perform required functions under stated conditions.
MTTR - Mean Time To Resolve, time spent in fixing a system.

Figure 6-20. *Did you know?*

In recent times SRE and DevOps have become extremely important and sought-after skills in organizations. Everyone has their own definition of what the role or responsibility of this team is, and there are various team structures in which these teams are structured. There is no universal definition of a DevOps engineer or an SRE, and there are overlaps in skill set and responsibilities. Let's try to capture the two roles, including the differences and overlaps between the two roles.

SRE and DevOps Structures

In the SRE team, it is expected that every team member is skilled on all areas and becomes multiskilled or E-shaped in terms of skills. In DevOps it is about different team members with different skills coming together to deliver an integrated development and operations experience with the help of culture, processes, best practices, tools, and technologies.

The team structure varies from company to company and in general has the following specialists:

- *Product owner*: This person is the interface between the business and the product and manages the product roadmap and strategy for the product.

- *Infra architect*: This person is responsible for the cloud and noncloud infrastructure architecture including networking, storage, compute, and other elements.

- *Software developer*: This person creates code and test cases, there may not be a separate testing team, and developers may double up as testers writing automated tests.

- *QA engineer*: This person is responsible for the overall quality of the product and ensuring the QA processes of third-party testing, etc., are handled.

- *Release manager*: This person is responsible for the release management function including release plans and scheduling.

- *Administrators (system and application)*: This person is in charge of monitoring, management, and patching activities along with automation for provisioning and deprovisioning of infrastructure and availability of these systems.

As can be seen from the previous roles, the sysadmin role morphs into the SME role in organizations where the strategy is to walk the SRE path. Also, when SREs are part of the DevOps teams, there may be some activities that are done by other teams and not the SRE team, especially releasing a deployment.

Tools and Technologies in DevOps and SRE Domain

Since there is an overlap between SRE and DevOps and since the way teams and individuals are structured around groups is different from organization to organization, the following skills are essential for both teams. The only difference will be that the resources in the SRE model may be cross-skilled across some of them, while in the DevOps model, the culture, best practices, and guiding principles will allow the DevOps team to seamlessly handle the entire spectrum of technologies required to deliver an end-to-end service. See Figure 6-21.

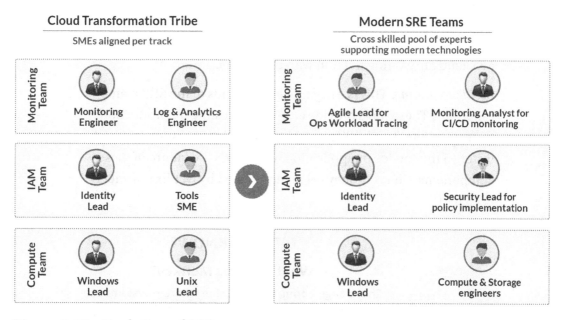

Figure 6-21. *Evolution of SREs*

Containers and microservices: Docker and Kubernetes services are available as SaaS offerings from various Cloud providers like AWS, GCP, and Azure.

Monitoring tools: Tools like Prometheus, Zabbix, etc., are important elements of the service that are required to deliver ongoing operations. Various organizations may be using tools from COTS vendors like CA Broadcom, IBM, Microfocus, BMC, Solarwinds, and Zenoss.

CI/CD/testing tools: Tools like Jenkins, Git, Gitlab, One Test Suite, Selenium, AppScan, Whitesource, SonarQube, Microsoft TFS, Azure DevOps, and other cloud-native DevOps tool chains along with deployment and configuration management tools like Ansible, Puppet, and Chef fall into this category.

Infrastructure as code (IaC): Native cloud technologies like Cloud Formation templates, Deployment Manager templates, and ARM templates along with third-party tools like Terraform, Puppet, Chef, and Ansible are the backbone of automation. Along with these, AI-driven COTS tools like DRYiCE iAutomate and DRYiCE MyCloud are gaining traction with customers.

Resilience testing: This is a key tool in the hands of the SRE teams especially. These tools provide end-to-end testing on production systems to test their resilience by bringing down components and testing if the service or application withstands the failure of these components. Chaos Money originally created by Netflix is a widely used tool.

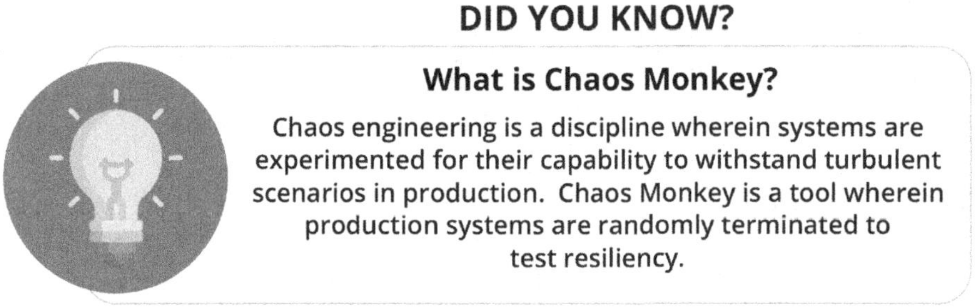

DID YOU KNOW?

What is Chaos Monkey?

Chaos engineering is a discipline wherein systems are experimented for their capability to withstand turbulent scenarios in production. Chaos Monkey is a tool wherein production systems are randomly terminated to test resiliency.

Figure 6-22. *Did you know?*

Balance Between Dev and Ops Work

When you move to a DevOps mode of operations and integrate the teams or make developers responsible for all kinds of operations, another challenge arises. The developers will now get overwhelmed with unplanned work, customer escalations, availability, and downtime of infrastructure and regular maintenance jobs. This may lead to dissatisfaction in the development teams, and the teams may also get distracted from the core job of developing features. Thus, SRE plays an important role here. They focus on the resilience aspects and also work on monitoring and ensuring the entire IT landscape from infrastructure to applications is up and running.

In this model, since the availability SLAs are well defined and there is an error budget defined, the focus of the SRE on availability and resilience ensures that prioritization is done systematically through metrics. Another point to note here is that the error budget or breaches of availability targets would automatically prioritize system stability over feature releases, and the focus of the team would be to ensure that the releases that may hamper availability and impact the metrics are planned and coordinated with the development teams.

An Agile-based Scrum backlog is used by the SRE teams for automation and engineering activities such as problem management and change management. Also, ITIL-based SLAs related to availability and prioritization using priority and severity (along with time to respond and resolve) are metrics used to prioritize the incidents happening in the IT landscape. This creates a balance between the two and ensures agility and speed while keeping the lights on and ensuring the services are available for the end consumers. The following method defines the priority:

- Pull things from the triage queue.

- If there are no triage items, work on the next item from the sprint backlog.

At first the teams may have a conflict between the SLA-driven workflow and the agile-based sprint work. Questions that you may find during the initial stages are "What if there is a lot of support work; how would we get time for sprint deliverables?" Once you are able to overcome the initial challenges, you will soon find that the work will balance out on a longer timeframe, and the teams will be able to complete the sprint tasks as well as take care of the flow of work. The flow of work becomes more predictable as the teams become familiar both with the technical environment and with the new process. Since the SRE sprints will include automation activities, you will slowly start seeing the benefits of this focused approach where the availability and performance issues become lesser and lesser. The problem management function typically takes a backseat in the incident management and service request management focused delivery gets the required attention in the SRE model and eliminates repeated work and repeated incidents.

Since the flow-based work is unpredictable and there are periods where there may not be any incidents or service requests to pull, the SRE teams are able to utilize the time for running the sprints for automation and service improvement.

Another important aspect to consider when mixing flow and sprint-based work is that if an engineer working on a sprint is interrupted, often then there is a waste of time for him to restart the work from wherever it was left, so some intelligent routing is necessary to balance the sprint work and workflow based on the availability of resources and the flow queues to reduce the number of interruptions that an engineer working on a sprint deliverable will face. The rotation of resources to carry more sprint work versus the flow is a technique to achieve this objective. Ultimately, the overall utilization of resources in this model will be much higher than with two different teams doing the sprint and the flow-based work, and the focus on continual service improvement will result in an accelerated path to maturity and high availability with fewer incidents.

In this model, you will achieve the following:

- SLAs for workflow improve along with other metrics like mean time to respond and resolve.

- Sprint velocity improves as teams are able to better predict the workload and plan.

- There are improved satisfaction scores for developers and administration teams.

- Customer satisfaction scores improve.

- There is a higher level of team motivation and collaboration.

Summary

All the frameworks covered in this chapter have a unique usage and adoption pattern. Any organization that intends to adopt one of these frameworks first needs to identify the framework that will best suit their needs. This is dependent on multiple factors such as team structure, distribution, composition, technology landscape, release cycle, agile competency, and understanding. Such an in-depth analysis helps organization make the right choice and then drive toward defining the roadmap for its adoption at the enterprise scale. This journey needs to have milestones and metrics to measure the adoption and success. Enterprises should also plan for trainings and mentoring for their teams so that they can avoid resistance. Teams should be made aware of the new engineering technologies like infrastructure as code, resiliency testing, monitoring and observability, and also DevOps-led tooling for CI/CD so that they feel their importance in the system and contribute in the transformation. Once the framework has been identified and teams start out on their new journey, they need to identify how they will operate. The new ways of working needs method definitions and process refinements. To work in agile infrastructure operations, we would need new team structures, roles and responsibilities, process changes, new ways of working, and tools and techniques. We will deep dive on these methods and their usage in the next few chapters.

CHAPTER 7

Using Agile for Infrastructure Operations

In this chapter, we will detail a step-by-step approach for adopting agile for infrastructure operations in an enterprise. The topics that will be covered in this chapter are as follows:

- The starting point

- Summarizing the transformation plan

We spoke about how the IT world is evolving and shifting from traditional operating structures to new agile structures in the infrastructure operations domain. We also looked at various agile frameworks and methods that are being adopted by enterprises that are upscaling their infrastructure operations teams to new roles and responsibilities. While agile is the way forward, the purpose is to provide a new way of operations that will enable and empower teams that in turn will deliver quickly in iterations. But, a key question you will have is, "where do you start from?" This is a question for organizations running complex and large infrastructure and cloud operations that want to move quickly into agile infrastructure operations to meet the ever-increasing demands of customers. Other reasons for such enterprises to move to a new model are moving up the maturity curve and getting benefits of higher availability and resilience while still saving on costs. Implementing agile infrastructure operations provides all of the previous benefits while also making the teams more collaborative, cohesive, productive, and motivated.

© Navin Sabharwal, Raminder Rathore, and Udita Agrawal 2022
N. Sabharwal et al., *Hands-On Guide to AgileOps*, https://doi.org/10.1007/978-1-4842-7505-4_7

The Starting Point

To being with, it is important to find where we stand in terms of the maturity of processes, functions, tools, and resources by verifying the effectiveness of current methods and processes. This is where self-assessments come to the rescue. After an assessment, it is time to write out a plan based on the current gaps and learnings and start the transition with small steps to begin with team-level advancements toward the new working methods. See Figure 7-1.

Where to Start From?

Figure 7-1. *Starting point for AgileOps*

But before all this, there needs to be need, commitment, and organizational buy-in for the following (see Figure 7-2):

- Agility is important, and every department in the organization should prepare for it.

- We need to ensure resiliency in our systems and be ready to fail and recover quickly.

- There is also a need to relook at the team size and the technologies at play.

- Focus on real-time performance analysis and agree to continuously monitor it.

- Encourage teams to embrace the new change and adopt agile ways of working.

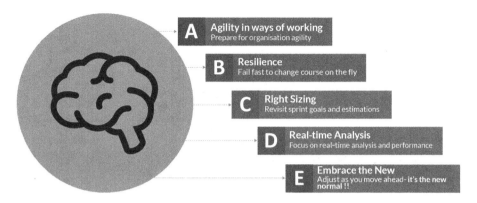

Figure 7-2. *Defining new ways of working*

Implementing AgileOps demands upskilling, better collaboration techniques, and investments in the right tools and technologies so that teams are ready to adopt and practice the cultural shift.

Let's look at some of the building blocks that will enable organizations to adopt agile culture and practices.

Adopting the Right Agile Framework and Methodology

Based on an organization's team structures, role definitions, responsibilities, technology platforms in use, etc., organizations should select the right agile framework as described in Chapter 6. The identification of the right framework is important and serves as the foundation block for the new journey. This framework can have teams running in different agile methods. While there are various agile methods available, both Scrum and Kanban have been the commonly used methods when it comes to software development and infrastructure operations. These methods provide visibility at the program level as well as the team level, and they foster the culture of "pulling work" rather than "pushing work." See Figure 7-3.

Kanban	Scrum
Visual boards	Fixed timeboxed sprints
Ideal for production operations	Ideal for development with fixed sprints
No mandate on standups	Standups are mandatory
Focus on cycle time	Focus on velocity
Changes can be made at any time	No changes allowed mid-sprint

Figure 7-3. *Agile models*

Just to recap, Scrum is a method suitable for teams that need to deliver work in fixed periodic intervals, and Kanban is suitable for operations teams where issues are to be resolved immediately. So, before we start on the agile journey, it is important to identify the right methodology for the team based on the deliverables from the team. If the team is to deliver work in fixed intervals called *sprints* that could be an application service or infrastructure as code, then Scrum is the right method. Both methods should be evaluated thoroughly. Teams can also adopt both methods; for example, 80 percent of the team focuses on operations tasks and adopts Kanban, while the other 20 percent of the team focuses on new work that is to be delivered every two weeks. Here Scrum is the ideal fit. The combination of Scrum and Kanban is called *scrumban*, which leverages the best of both methods.

It is important that teams are also mentored on using these methods in the right way. Just adopting the method for its namesake will not help. It has to be practiced in totality. It is not about renaming existing meetings as standups and Scrum meetings but changing the culture of an organization using proven organizational change management techniques and practices. Expecting cultural change in a short span of time is unrealistic; hence, we need to plan this change in a stepwise fashion. Teams need to "pull" work instead of "push." They need to be encouraged to become accountable for the work items and ensure that they get delivered without any showstoppers. This is where the culture of learning and nurturing agile methods becomes important. We need to understand that the first step is unlearning the culture, processes, and ways of working and then move on to learn the new culture and ways of working; since it involves not technology but people, it is a slow process. We need to define a step-by-step journey where we can get people to implement new ways of working and achieve a higher level of maturity.

For an IT operations teams where tickets are submitted in tools like ServiceNow or BMC Remedy or Atlassian Jira, etc., and they get routed to team leads who then assign the tickets to respective specialist for resolution, Kanban is an ideal method. In comparison to the traditional ops where tickets are pushed, in Kanban the tickets are picked up by the team specialists. This culture shift demands cross-skilling within the teams so that the knowledge is not restricted to a set of specialists. In fact, the knowledge is available with the team. Some organizations call these cross-skilled specialists *site reliability engineers* and are also renaming their groups as *squads*. However, just renaming a team or a set of functions to a different name doesn't make operations agile; there has to be a step-by-step journey to achieve maturity in agile methods and practices.

So, what all is needed to adopt and implement agile?

Identifying the Agile Methodology

Assuming that the framework has been selected, the agile method needs to be shortlisted. We covered the agile methods in detail in Chapter 5. Teams should evaluate the right method that will suit their organizational needs based on their current level of maturity, team composition, outsourced versus insourced environment, and other parameters. The commonly used methods are Scrum, Kanban, and the hybrid version called scrumban. Based on the current working style and expectations, the right method should be selected for the team. Organizations can pilot a method with one team, evaluate its efficiency, and then later expand. Once teams on the ground get used to the agile working style, then this can easily scale at the enterprise level. Large and complex organizations may end up with a mix of agile methods in different departments, geographies, or parts of the organization. Efforts should be made to build synergies and common best practices with some level of central guidance so that the differences are minimal and are based on the genuine needs of a particular department rather than because of personal preferences. We need to start small and then expand; there may be challenges on the way. When that happens, go back to the drawing board to use the Agile Manifesto, principles, and cultural guidance from DevOps and lean and you will be able to solve these challenges.

Identifying Tools for Implementation

Similar to the methods and frameworks, multiple tools are available that can be leveraged to help teams practice agile ceremonies, track work, have work visibility, etc. Table 7-1 describes the key features. See Figure 7-4.

Table 7-1. *Agile Project Management Tools*

Vendor	Tool	Key Features
Atlassian	Jira Agile	• Offers templates for agile project adoption • Integrates with other Atlassian tools like BitBucket for version control, Bamboo for continuous integration and deployment, HipChat for collaboration, Confluence for documentation, etc. • Provides excellent reporting and dashboarding capabilities • Available as on-premise as well as SaaS solution
Collabnet	VersionOne	• Designed for agile and lean implementation • Offers the openAgile API to integrate with other tools • An enterprise application lifecycle management tool
Planview	Leankit	• Implements Kanban • Emphasizes lean principles • Visually communicates blocked work and identifies process bottlenecks through effective workflows • Offers integrations with other enterprise-grade tools like ITSM, PPM, etc.

DID YOU KNOW?

NASA's Jet Propulsion Lab (a lab responsible to test emerging rocket technologies and developing robotic spacecraft) uses Atlassian products to build software for flight mission planning and also modeling data that is transferred between satellites and Mars.

Figure 7-4. *Did you know?*

Identifying the Need for Extended Integration

While there are stand-alone tools for agile management, it is important that this tool integrates with other tools that are used in product development. For example, in most organizations, development teams use Jira, and their operations teams use ServiceNow. To bridge the gap between both these teams, we need to ideate on how to stitch the process gaps and encourage teams to look at integrated dashboards and workloads. This is possible if both these tools are integrated, bringing in bidirectional traceability. Both teams have visibility and share common processes as well. Yet another use case is wherein stories are to be linked with code files. If the source code is stored in tools like Git or BitBucket, then this definitely calls for an integration between the tools. In the end, product teams get end-to-end visibility of their work items. See Figure 7-5.

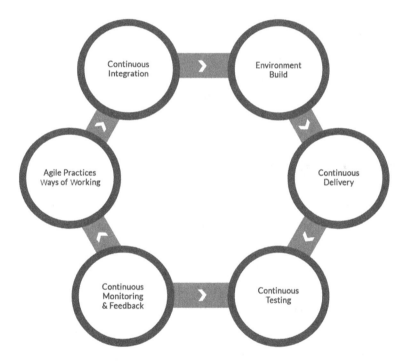

Figure 7-5. *End-to-end integration between tools*

Upgrading Teams on Using the Agile Approach

Teams need to be coached when adopting an agile method or tool. It is important that teams are supervised and mentored by an experienced agile coach who helps them use the tools effectively and efficiently. Certified specialists in agile and DevOps will serve as excellent coaches or mentors for the teams. Such experts also help in articulating the roadmap, measuring the maturity, and continuously monitoring the agile adoption. Since there is little guidance available on using agile for cloud operations and integrating with DevOps and site reliability engineering, there may be gaps in skills, but this book can act as a best-practice guide for you to implement your plans.

Redefining Team Roles and Responsibilities

New methods and frameworks may meet resistance from employees, and this can be softened with the help of organizational change management techniques and practices and the appreciation of the fact that the journey toward agile is a team effort. New roles should be introduced within the team to increase enthusiasm. Team members should be given a chance to call out their interests and move to new roles. New responsibilities will encourage team members and create excitement. As an example in the infrastructure operations space, the service request manager can move to a product owner role with training of best practices for using agile in operations. With new roles, the concepts of self-management and transparency should be adopted as these are the core principles of agile.

Nurturing the Culture of "Pulling Work"

Another aspect of strengthening agile practices is the art wherein team members pull work instead of waiting for someone to give them work. This is the key difference in the way of working between traditional models and agile. For ages, team hierarchies were created that followed a top-to-bottom approach. In the agile world, hierarchies should be minimized, and any corporate structures should motivate teams toward adopting the change. The target should be to slowly evolve into teams that are self-sustaining.

Baselining the Initial Cycle Time and Related Metrics

If agile is a journey, then we need to track the progress of this journey. When combined with DevOps and site reliability practices, this becomes a journey for continuous improvement. To track such progress, self-assessment needs to be done regularly. This can be done at the team or product or enterprise level. At the team level, we need metrics, and this is where we should baseline metrics and keep revisiting them frequently to see if the team is benefitting from the adoption and if there is a need to change course. These metrics can include simple measurements such as the number of work items or the time taken to implement a story. If the number of work items doesn't increase over a period of time, then this may indicate that either the team is not able to take the load or something needs correction. A detailed analysis of the process following the lean principles will help in identifying root causes and in taking corrective action.

Figure 7-6 explains a sample way to evaluate the progress of a team running in Scrum mode. This team manages four applications, and each has features, stories, and bugs. Stories further have its associated tasks and complexities. To begin with, teams can capture the metrics every two months against a set of team members. This data helps to analyze if the number of features and story points being delivered is increasing or not, which means the team is able to absorb more work since they are gaining experience. On average, if the number of features and story points delivered is increasing with the same team size but the number of bugs is decreasing, then this indicates that the team is able to deliver more with improved quality. This is also called the team *throughput/ velocity*, and it should be monitored for continuous improvement. If the throughput/ velocity is not improving, then the Scrum master should analyze the reasons and plan for appropriate steps in consultation with the product owner. There could be various reasons that affect a team's throughput/velocity like limited competency or dependencies, complexity of work, etc.

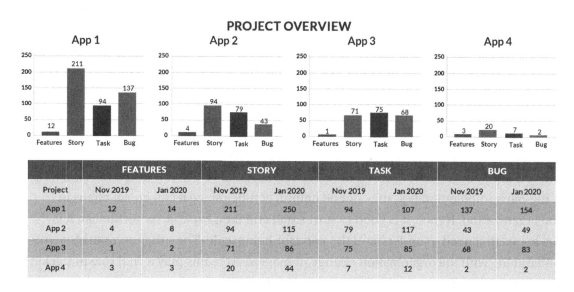

	FEATURES		STORY		TASK		BUG	
Project	Nov 2019	Jan 2020	Nov 2019	Jan 2020	Nov 2019	Jan 2020	Nov 2019	Jan 2020
App 1	12	14	211	250	94	107	137	154
App 2	4	8	94	115	79	117	43	49
App 3	1	2	71	86	75	85	68	83
App 4	3	3	20	44	7	12	2	2

Figure 7-6. *Sample metrics tracking*

Identifying Candidates for Self-Servicing

While the teams gear up for the new norm, it is important to also set down the goals and vision statement for the team. A mission statement defines the organization's work, objective, and its approach to follow it. A vision statement describes the desired future of the organization. For an operations team, the vision and mission statement could include elements from availability, resilience, agility, security, cost of operations, customer satisfaction, business growth, etc. The mission is something that needs to be accomplished; thus, the broader mission needs to be translated to granular use cases that form the backlog for the agile operations team. See Figure 7-7.

USE CASE #1	**USE CASE #2**	**USE CASE #3**
Developers should be able to provision dev environments themselves	Testers should be able to spin and decommission test environments on demand	Developers should be able to trigger CI pipeline

Figure 7-7. *Sample use cases*

Creating Team Dashboards for Visibility

When a coach joins the team, they need to set up the initial set of reports and dashboards for the team to refer to and set a baselines. These dashboards should reflect real-time project statistics and help the team to pull work. The metrics that are baselined should be made visible on these dashboards. Dashboards can be layered out as well to address different stakeholders. For example, tools like Confluence can be leveraged to create and display program and team-level dashboards. These dashboards also serve as quick reference points in various ceremonies.

Piloting and Extending the Approach

A big-bang implementation may not be helpful at times since it can create chaos in the organization. Hence, it is good to start small and then expand. Nevertheless, it is the teams that need to understand the need for being agile. The program management office along with the organization change management teams play a vital role in tracking the transformation program and extending its realm. This is where organizations can identify a group that should be piloted first, and then based on the learnings, the practices are extended to other teams. The pilot always acts as a learning platform for other teams. Selecting the pilot team is also a key step toward defining the success for the transformation. Avoid selecting a team that is working on a critical environment or an application. Select a low to medium-level team that has time to upscale and adopt the new norms of working. The learnings from this pilot should be documented and showcased in the organization, and other teams can see the success and start the journey toward becoming agile.

Continuously Measuring Metrics and Replanning

The initial time period will have hurdles for the team, but to ensure that the team runs on the right track, the coaches should revisit what was started and how the team is evolving. This will help them change the course of action as needed and also identify missing gaps and learn from these gaps. Feedback from other teams and management are also key to observing the performance. As the changes are being revisited, the scope should not be just on tools and automation; it should also look at areas that can be streamlined, in other words, areas wherein a team needs skilling.

Summarizing the Transformation Plan

The steps mentioned earlier can be rolled out in three phases, as shown in Figure 7-8.

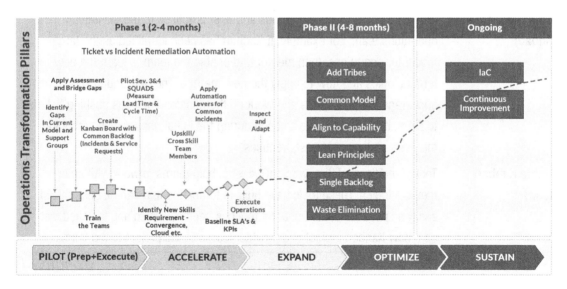

Figure 7-8. *Phased-wise transformation plan*

Phase 1: Pilot and Accelerate

This initial phase is a foundation pillar that serves as the building block. It usually stretches between two to four months, but this may get extended depending on multiple factors. To ensure that this phase is managed and implemented successfully, it is important that the right team for piloting is identified, and the team is mentored with all the required skills and practices. See Table 7-2.

Table 7-2. *Milestones*

Milestone	Description
Identify gaps	Benchmark the current support model and ways of working in the operations area. Analyze on how teams collaborate, what processes and tools are leveraged, and what hinders faster delivery. The identified gaps across people, process, and tools are consolidated, and these act as important inputs to draft a roadmap for continuous improvement that gets driven through agility.
Apply assessment	Create a roadmap that addresses the gaps. Identify a team that should be piloted with the new agile model. These new teams will be called *squads*. It is important that the roadmap focuses on bridging the gaps that have been assessed.
Train the team (squad)	Provide training on agile methods and best practices to the identified operations team. For example, if Kanban has been identified as the target model for operations, then mentor and enable the team to learn the new terminologies and how to apply the new method. The new squad should be encouraged to pull tickets and work on them instead of leads pushing tickets to them. It is good to have a coach during the initial phases who can guide the team and suggest best practices.
Create Kanban board	Tools like Atlassian Jira, VersionOne, etc., help teams to work with agile methodologies. These tools have built-in templates that can be customized easily as per the needs. Once the tool has been identified and installed, set up a new Kanban project and provide access to the project to the team.

(continued)

Table 7-2. (*continued*)

Milestone	Description
Pilot severity 3 and 4 tickets	Once the squad is ready to operate in agile mode, initiate the new model for severity 3 and 4 incidents or service requests. As tickets get into the backlog, the squad will be able to view the backlog and pull tickets/incidents based on their bandwidth. The coach or lead can drive the flow of tickets with the team and observe areas that need attention like members facing issues in moving tickets from one state to another or members having issues in pulling tickets and understanding the new process.
Identify new skills	As the new squad team learns to work in the new working model, leads get to know the team velocity and identify areas where the squad needs to improvise. There could be scenarios wherein organizations moving to the cloud also need to be upskilled to support the new platform; hence, along with agile methods, teams should be trained on new technologies like the cloud and infrastructure as code.
Cross-skill	As squads get upskilled, they also need to be cross-skilled. For instance, team members should understand the complete process flow on how infrastructure is set up and how related components are created and tracked. Another example is that there could be multiskilled resources particularly in the cloud computing domain where each resource can be cross-skilled in cloud operations, cloud architecture, cloud deployment, networking, and platforms.
Apply automation	One best practice to drive agility in infrastructure operations is to automate whatever is possible. Adopting infrastructure as code is a good start that standardizes the process for infrastructure deployments and avoids any manual errors during setup and foundation build. Leverage out-of-box tools that speed up the automation process.

(*continued*)

Table 7-2. (*continued*)

Milestone	Description
Baseline SLAs and KPIs	To measure success, it is important to note the path that was chosen. To track agile adoption, it is necessary that both SLAs and metrics are identified and baselined. These values should be regularly visited to ensure that there is an improvement with the implementation of the new method. For example, to begin with, baseline the lead time taken to solve a ticket and then track this lead time frequently to see if this is improving. If earlier it was eight hours, then whether it is being reduced. Obviously, there will be some caveats like complexity and type of the tickets. But measuring metrics periodically helps teams to review their progress on the path toward automation and agility.
Execute ops in new model	Once the pilot model matures, then extend this new working model for other ticket categories. The team may continue to operate with the older method in parallel for some more time until they switch over to the new model. Such a working model is called Bimodal IT Operations - where the traditional and the new working models exist together for sometime.
Inspect and adapt	Continuous feedback is an essential part of this journey. As the team gets used to the new method, metrics, and ways of working, it is important to analyze and get their feedback on what works best and what doesn't, what needs to be corrected, and what should be added. This becomes a good case study for the rest of the teams that can refer, learn, and scale accordingly.

Phase 2: Expand and Optimize

Once the pilot is successful with one team, it is time for it to be extended to other operations teams. In fact, the pilot team serves as an excellent medium for others to understand the pros and cons of agile operations. As the name suggests, this phase focuses on extending the new ways of working to other teams and checks on areas that can be optimized. Optimization may be done by adopting the right tools and automation. This phase usually extends between four to eight months but may change based on the team strength and capacity. The key practices in Table 7-3 are added and matured.

Table 7-3. *Key Practices*

Focus Area	Description
Add tribes	In phase 1, we define the squad teams; these are self-organizing teams. When similar squad teams work together, they form a tribe. So, a tribe is a collection of squads. As the methodology extends to other teams, it is important to define a new team structure with roles and responsibilities.
Define a common model	Collaborative team efforts lead to agile success. As teams scale on agile methods and define new team structures (squads, tribes, chapters, etc.), it is essential that they share a common model for reference. This helps in bringing teams together and fosters a culture of learning. The model of operations should be a simplified version that is easy for teams to adopt and scale.
Align teams with capabilities	Introduce tribes in other areas and align them with capabilities for quick response times. Continuous feedback from capabilities will enable tribes to improvise as needed.
Adopt lean principles	As more and more teams adopt agile and implement automation, there is a need to embrace lean principles. The five principles of lean (define value, map to value stream, create flow, establish pull, and pursue perfection) focus on generating value. Tools like HCL Accelerate can be leveraged for value stream management.
Adopt a single backlog	Initially when squads are onboarded, each will have their own backlog. But as tribes are formed and teams get cross-skilled, leads and coaches should aim to have a common backlog. For example, there is one common backlog for one tribe.
Eliminate waste	As lean principles get implemented, waste has to be removed. This is where automation plays a crucial role. Leads should monitor areas that if automated would benefit them. Tracking waste acts as another factor for driving success in the agile adoption.

Phase 3: Sustainment

The last phase is an ongoing phase—a phase for continuous learning and improvements. This phase is about matured cross-skilled teams that are highly efficient. While the team now has matured on the infrastructure and cloud operations, the same team should expand their horizons and look at automation opportunities that facilitate speed and resilience. They slowly need to identify more squad teams and create new roles and responsibilities.

The following key factors drive this phase toward maturity with continuous improvements:

- *Self-service*: Teams can scale up and down environments with infrastructure as code templates. This is like when testers are empowered to build and decommission test environments in their pipelines without being dependent on operations teams to enable environments. This reduces wait time to test and deploy new features.

- *Zero-touch deployments*: These are made possible by end-to-end automation of CI/CD pipelines. Teams should be encouraged to practice pipeline deployments in production rather than manual deployments. An automated deployment not only avoids erroneous actions but also speeds up delivery time and shortens feedback loops. This frees the team to focus on innovative areas such as strengthening security and increasing coverage on testing, compliance, and guardrails.

- *Standardization and optimization*: As more and more opportunities are identified and implemented with automation, teams become more efficient, processes get more optimized, and standardized teams emphasize delivering reliable and resilient systems.

- *Continuous assessments*: Remember when we spoke about benchmarking the team status before getting started? So, we have the initial metrics, and now we should re-assess. The team needs to collect feedback on how it has performed and how it can improve. An assessment in this case is helpful; it enables teams to revisit their team structure, process workflows, methodologies, metrics, and skill levels. This helps them to identify and automate new opportunities to increase efficiency and update the course of action as required. Enterprises should adopt an assessment plan that is baselined and revisited regularly, say, every six months. Later, every iteration of this assessment is scored and then compared with the previous rating or score.

Figure 7-9 displays a sample assessment that has five stages, and each stage gets tagged with a set of defined practices. For example, a team assesses and baselines itself at Level 1 (since it is completely traditional). But after six months, they progress toward

Level 2 and slowly keep progressing thereafter. The Initializing phase at Level 2 indicates that everyone in the team knows the agile concepts and understands its significance as well as have started leveraging agile methods like using Scrum boards, ceremonies, etc. Such an assessment should be carried out regularly to capture the current maturity levels and help teams to plan for changes.

- Conduct workshops to mentor on the purpose of being agile and on adopting automation for improving team performance.

- Revisit the organization roadmap and milestones.

- Plan for new competency programs.

- Identify applications that need to be modernized.

- Invest in new tools and automation.

- Standardize the tools platform across the lifecycle.

- Define an end-to-end integration and pipeline strategy.

- Identify processes for automation and optimization.

- Extend support and communication to larger groups.

- Track and improve the team's throughput/cycle time and other metrics.

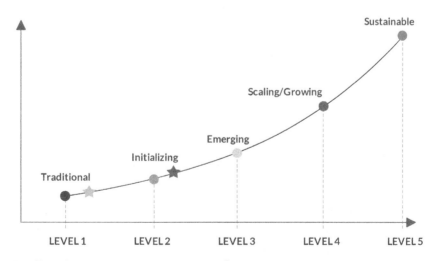

Figure 7-9. *Continuous assessment sample output*

Table 7-4 describes the maturity assessment levels.

Table 7-4. *Maturity Assessment Levels*

Level	Name	Key Features
1	Traditional	• Waterfall approach • Siloed and reactive teams • Multiple tools with no/limited integration
2	Initializing	• Understand agile and related concepts • Identify standard tools for integration • Teams start practicing agile ceremonies
3	Emerging	• Getting started with pipeline development • Baseline metrics for team performance • Basic infrastructure operations automated
4	Scaling/Growing	• Define service catalog • Identify use cases for automation • Automated delivery pipeline • Collaborative and proactive teams • Extend infrastructure as code with development pipelines
5	Sustainable	• Self-service catalog publication • Self-remediation • Continuous assessment and improvement • Moving toward AIOps

Summary

A journey to agile infrastructure operations is a planned, step-by-step process of moving teams toward agility, automation, and resiliency. A successful plan should embed motivation in teams and scale up as they grow. So, it is good to pilot a few teams first and then extend this to other teams in the operations domain. Of course, there will be failures that are indicators that the plan needs a change. There could be multiple phases driving the agile plan, but this should be designed based on the organization charter and expectations. Organizations should aim to achieve the following set of goals:

- Short-lived iteration-based workloads

- Standardization and optimization

- Self-service

- Automation

- Continuous monitoring and collecting feedback for growth

Assuming that the infrastructure operations team has adopted Kanban and the new operating model is moving forward on the maturity curve, we need to analyze and move toward the next step in the transformation journey. Now is the time where we need to introduce infrastructure as code and enable the design and integration of infrastructure pipelines with application pipelines. This step can be done in sequence or can be done in parallel based on the team bandwidth. We will now deep dive into the concepts of infrastructure as code and understand the key building blocks that are needed for using the agile-Scrum method.

CHAPTER 8

Moving to Agile with Infrastructure as Code

In this chapter, we will discuss how to get started on infrastructure as code. The topics that will be covered in this chapter are as follows:

- Getting started with infrastructure as code using Scrum

- Estimating stories

- Defining acceptance criteria

- An infrastructure build example

- Tools pipeline

- Infrastructure as code example

- Integrating infrastructure as code (IaC) with development pipelines

- Extending the IaC example

- Key agile practices while adopting IaC using Scrum

The birth of infrastructure as code has been one of the transforming trends in the IT industry in the past decade. The thought process behind this trend is that if applications can be autodeployed, then why can't infrastructure? Why is it that the servers have to be built and configured manually? As more and more organizations move to the cloud, the expectation is to speed up deliveries, and infrastructure as code plays a crucial role in this adoption.

> *Infrastructure as code (IaC) is the process of managing and provisioning computers through machine-readable definition files, rather than physical hardware configuration or interactive configuration tools.*
>
> —Definition from Wikipedia

© Navin Sabharwal, Raminder Rathore, and Udita Agrawal 2022
N. Sabharwal et al., *Hands-On Guide to AgileOps*, https://doi.org/10.1007/978-1-4842-7505-4_8

The traditional operating model had to change, and this gave rise to many configuration tools that helped organizations to adopt infrastructure as code. This also paved the way for the IT operations team to upscale to new technologies like Chef, Puppet, Ansible, Terraform, etc. Additionally, many cloud providers offer native infrastructure as code tools (like AWS CFN, Google SDKs, Azure ARM templates, etc.). There are also enterprise cloud lifecycle management tools such as DRYiCE MyCloud that make the journey to infrastructure as code faster. This helps teams to adapt quickly and move toward infrastructure automation through code.

It also helps IT operations to become agile and deliver flexible as well as reliable services. Setting up a new infrastructure through code not only creates the infrastructure for deploying applications, but also creates the supporting and mandatory components such as networks, firewalls, storage, etc. A central repository is created that versions all the code that is comprised of scripts, templates, and policies. These scripts are triggered directly or are called through orchestration tools like Jenkins, TeamCity, etc., and are version controlled using tools like Git, GitHub, etc. In fact, in some organizations, these repositories are shared with development teams to write code for building new infrastructure. This is an excellent medium that brings the development and operations teams together. See Figure 8-1.

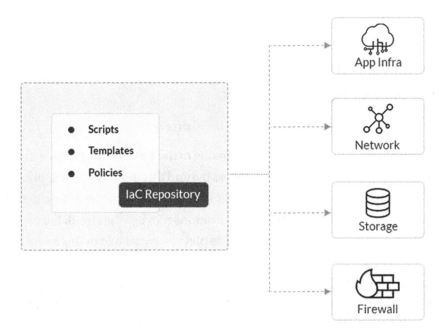

Figure 8-1. *Controlling and managing infrastructure with IaC*

Another faster approach to achieve this in the cloud world is to use cloud lifecycle management tools, which integrate with the existing set of processes that are based on ITIL as well as provide capabilities for infrastructure as code through easy-to-use interfaces and out-of-the-box integration with multiple cloud providers and templates. Tools like DRYiCE MyCloud help organizations achieve infrastructure as code with minimal setup time and reduce the time to market. The MyCloud platform supports VMware, SCVMM, AWS, Azure, and GCP environments and integrates with IT service management, service catalog, monitoring, and management tools along with CI/CD tools to provide integration between the development and operations teams.

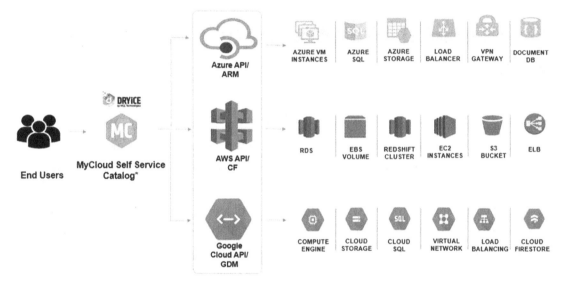

Figure 8-2. *HCL DRYiCE MyCloud, CLM tool*

Organizations that manage and control infrastructure through code can save tremendous amount of efforts with automation and also avoid human errors. Manipulating infrastructure directly through code also allows teams to keep track of who made the changes, when these changes were made, and what components were modified. As the infrastructure matures, the teams also implement policies to ensure that there are no manual changes being done in the infrastructure. If a manual change is being executed, the tool reverts those changes and alerts the administrators about this change.

Table 8-1. *Benefits of IaC*

Benefits with Infrastructure as Code
Quick time to market—servers deployed instantly
Foster collaboration—bridges gaps between teams
Standardize operating methodology—minimizing risk
Traceability—audit and track every component
Optimize cost—reduce operational expenditure

Getting Started with Infrastructure as Code Using Scrum

The journey toward infrastructure as code starts by building a new team. The team is typically called the automation or DevOps or IaC team. The role of this team is to use infrastructure as code tools and to collaborate with development teams to build new automation use cases. Scrum is an ideal agile methodology for teams that are into building components. This DevOps/automation team defines stories in the backlog that are discussed and prioritized by the team after discussions with the stakeholders. They build infrastructure pipelines that are made available as a catalog service and have the flexibility to be integrated with the development pipeline. The infrastructure components are delivered in a modularized fashion. The team first creates epics that are reviewed, prioritized, and budgeted, and these are later broken down to features/stories that run in sprints. The teams practice Scrum ceremonies and also frequently deliver a minimum viable product (MVP) toward the sprint end. This MVP is demonstrated at the end of the sprint. Any issues in the MVP or enhancements are placed back into the backlog. See Figure 8-3.

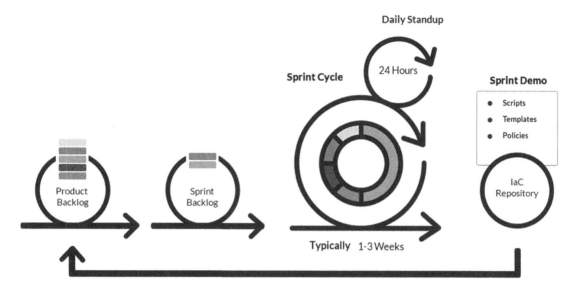

Figure 8-3. *Planning IaC through Scrum*

To get started on this journey, the first step is to upskill the team on the new methodology and make the team members comfortable with adopting Scrum. New role definitions are created that are aligned to the agile process like Scrum master, product owner, AgileOps Scrum team, etc. The product owner is responsible for defining the requirements and is the interface between the business, customers, application development teams, and the AgileOps Scrum team. The end goal for this team is to standardize and automate the infrastructure in an agile manner. As the team gets ready to work in Scrum mode, a platform is also identified wherein the epics and stories will be created, updated, and tracked. It is important that the team learns to operate this tool and are able to visualize the product journey.

Let's take a quick look at the key terminologies in this structure; see Table 8-2.

Table 8-2. *Scrum Terminology*

Scrum Terminology	Description
Product backlog	This comprises epics and stories for building infrastructure components. These items are discussed with key stakeholders and then documented in this backlog.
Sprint backlog	Before the start of every sprint, high-priority user stories are identified and moved to the sprint backlog. The stories in this backlog are the ones that will be implemented by the team.
Daily standup	As the sprint progresses, each day the team meets for 15 to 20 minutes to discuss their workload and risks that need attention.
Sprint cycle	Every sprint has a duration; some teams run in sprints of two weeks, while a few run a sprint for three weeks. But once this duration is decided on, teams should not be allowed to change it. Since there is little empirical data on infrastructure operations sprints, you need to tweak the sprint duration based on the projects and team size and skills.
Sprint demo	At the end of the sprint, the developed product or script is run by the key stakeholders. Any defects or issues are noted and placed back in the backlog.

A good practice while getting started with Scrum is to start with sprint 0, which acts as a litmus test for the team. The team also gets to revisit the duration of the sprint as well as the number of stories that they can deliver in a sprint. For example, the team decides to have a sprint cycle for two weeks with seven members. They identify a few stories and by the end of the sprint realize that two weeks for the sprint cycle is not sufficient. They either need to reduce the number of stories in a sprint or increase the sprint cycle to three weeks. After the completion of sprint 0, the successive sprints should stick to these principles. It is important that the traceability between requirement types (epics, features, stories) is defined. Teams need to agree on the different requirement types that they would need. While some have four types, there are others who stick to just three levels like epics, stories, and tasks, and that suffices their journey. Tools like Azure DevOps, JIRA, etc., provide this capability to state these different requirement types and also create custom types. In a portfolio model, themes are created at the portfolio level that are then further broken down into epics, features, stories, and tasks that spread across the program and team levels. See Figure 8-4.

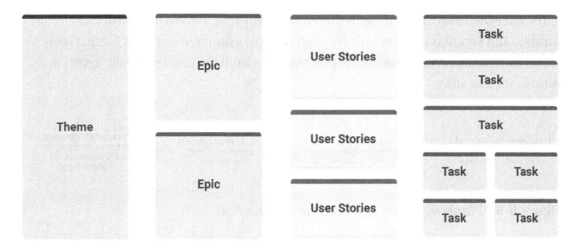

Figure 8-4. *Agile components*

Another success factor for sprint delivery is making the right estimations. It is the team that collectively estimates the stories that are to be delivered, but leveraging the right techniques makes a key difference. These estimations are done during the sprint planning meeting. Each team member shares their view on the estimates, and a collective decision is made. At the end of the sprint planning meeting, the team needs to ensure that all the stories are reviewed and ready for implementation, and each story is estimated and linked with an epic or parent entity. The Scrum master facilitates the team by handholding them on the agile best practices in the initial phases. The Scrum master and team check if everyone in the team has stories to be addressed and no member is left behind. Emphasis is also made on ensuring there is enough capacity to complete the stories and they do not spill onto the next sprint.

Estimating Stories

Various methods are available that can be used to estimate stories. Some of the commonly used techniques are T-shirt sizing (XS for extra small, S for small, M for medium, L for large, XL for extra-large), numeric sizing (from 1 to 10), Fibonacci series (1, 2, 3, 5, 8, …), etc. To run these techniques, there are processes available that help teams to get to the closest estimates possible. Methods like Planning Poker can help teams to pick the right effort sizing in a collaborative manner (see Figure 8-5). This method is based on the team's mutual consensus. During the sprint planning session, each team member reads a common story and shares their estimates using numbered cards. They then share their reasons on how and why they arrived at a particular number. The Scrum master records the high and low estimated numbers for that story (for all the members) and repeats the process again until the team mutually agrees at a number for that story.

Figure 8-5. *Planning Poker, story estimation method*

Another commonly used method, mostly leveraged by development teams, is the functional point analysis (FPA) method wherein the functions are tagged with function points based on their complexity, and it includes testing efforts as well. For example, an application has four key functions that are to be either coded or tested like user interface, business logic, database connections, and testing. Each of these functions has points defined based on their complexity (as low, medium, high, and complex). See Figure 8-6.

User Interface	Business Logic	Database Interaction	Testing Scope
Low = 1 Medium = 2 High = 3 Complex = 4	Low = 1 Medium = 2 High = 3 Complex = 4	Low = 1 Medium = 2 High = 3 Complex = 4	Low = 1 Medium = 2 High = 3 Complex = 4

Figure 8-6. *Sample functional point analysis*

For infrastructure-driven stories, T-shirt sizing is the recommended technique that is easy to adopt and practice. Each T-shirt size depicts the complexity level. For example, a small-sized story means it can be developed quickly and is simple. On the other hand, M or L indicates that the story is more complex than the S-sized one and needs more development time. These sizes are linked with the Fibonacci series shown in Table 8-3.

Table 8-3. *T-Shirt Sizes and Equivalent Story Points*

Size	Description	Story Point
X-Small	Deliverable in a very short timeframe and very simple.	1
Small	Deliverable in a short timeframe and simple.	3
Medium	Deliverable in the scope of a release and is less complex.	5
Large	Potentially deliverable in the scope of a release and is complex.	8
X-Large	Very big, but generally understood. Needs further breakdown over several releases and is very complex.	13
XXL	Very big and uncertain area. Needs further breakdown into something manageable over various releases and is extremely complex.	21

We have the XL and XXL T-shirt sizes, but they should be avoided because a sprint size is two to three weeks and it will be difficult to complete these stories in one sprint. Therefore, the XL and XXL user stories should be broken down into multiple S, M, or L user stories.

Let's assume this sample user story:

As an admin, I should be able to monitor the CPU utilization of the server and generate alerts so that I can proactively rectify the problem.

To estimate this story, the following should be thought through:

- Understand the scope, what is needed.

- Clarify the end product, which is a script or a playbook.

- Create tasks for this story that need to be performed. This could be getting access to some tool, server, etc., for monitoring its CPU utilization.

- Provide estimates. If tools integration is in place, then only the script needs to be developed and tested. Then the sizing can be S or M based on how many OSs the script needs to cater to.

Note   Remember that every story should be independent, simple, and testable. Initially, teams may shy away from the estimation processes, but with the right training and mentorship, the teams will learn the methodology and realize the benefits. After all, this is needed for effective capacity planning.

Defining Acceptance Criteria

Another important aspect of agile stories is to define the acceptance criteria. This means that if a user story is to be moved ahead or is considered complete, then it has to be thoroughly tested. This is made possible by defining acceptance criteria. This can happen either at the epic level or at the story level. In tools like JIRA, you can define fields that prompts the users/business analysts to mention this list of acceptance criteria. If the result for all the listed criteria is true, then this means that the story can move ahead. Testing should include functional as well as nonfunctional areas. The golden rule is that each story should be linked with at least one acceptance criteria. Each criterion is written in the format "given-when-then" that mentions the scenario and the expected result. It is good practice to build acceptance criteria with user stories as they are built.

Table 8-4 shows a sample user story.

Table 8-4. *Sample User Story*

Story	Acceptance Criteria
As a: System administrator **I want to:** Integrate tool 1 with tool 2 through a REST API module **So that:** Alert notifications are visible and efficiently managed.	**Best Case:** **Given:** Tool 1 is integrated with Tool 2. **When:** A REST API is used. **Then:** Notifications are visible to the system administrator. **Worst Case:** **Given:** Integrations for Tool 1 and Tool 2 are not active. **When:** A REST API is deactivated/not working. **Then:** The system administrator is updated about the disintegration. **Nonfunctional Case:** **Given:** Tool 1 and tool 2 are integrated. **When:** A REST API is used. **Then:** Notifications should be pushed every one minute.

An Infrastructure Build Example

Let's look at an example of an epic that states the need for provisioning basic infrastructure like RHEL Linux using infrastructure as code. This epic is a big requirement that is broken down into stories, and each story is well thought through and estimated.

There are various methods available to write effective stories; Figure 8-7 shows the most common one.

User Stories

As a _____

I need _____

So that _____

Figure 8-7. *User story format*

The idea is to state the user persona who needs to run an activity for a specific purpose. It is important that teams understand that while agile states "working software over comprehensive documentation," there has to be some minimum documentation to support the implementation. A clear explanation of a need effectively helps to track changes in the future. This is an area where the InfraOps teams needs coaching. They may find that such documentation can be time-consuming. A coach can help to train these teams and also enable them to implement the technique in the right way. For example, an epic (high-level requirement) has been created called "Provision basic infra." Underneath this epic, the team creates the associated user stories. Each story is an independent functionality against which the team will build an automation. The team also spends time to estimate each story and ensure that it is well tested and deployed on time.

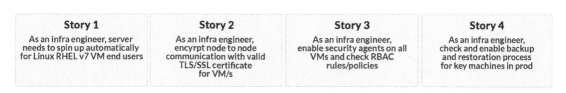

Story 1	Story 2	Story 3	Story 4
As an infra engineer, server needs to spin up automatically for Linux RHEL v7 VM end users	As an infra engineer, encyrpt node to node communication with valid TLS/SSL certificate for VM/s	As an infra engineer, enable security agents on all VMs and check RBAC rules/policies	As an infra engineer, check and enable backup and restoration process for key machines in prod

Figure 8-8. *Examples of IaC epic and related stories*

As teams evolve and get used to the Scrum methodology, they also learn to estimate the stories effectively and become more proficient. Having an agile practitioner or a coach accelerates the adoption of agile method and practices. This coach works with agile leads and the team and guides them on how to write effective stories, perform estimations, track team progress through dashboards, and enable teams to identify opportunities for improvement and automation.

Tools Pipeline

Another important element of change is that the lifecycle of building an infrastructure component whether it is a VM or a firewall or installing a security agent should practice CI/CD like how it is practiced in the application world. This means that like an application pipeline, an infrastructure pipeline should be built. Hence, every time new code is written or modified, the infrastructure pipeline gets triggered and runs through automated build process, unit testing, code coverage, and checks for security vulnerabilities. CI/CD automation is possible with the help of automated tools that are linked to an orchestrator like Jenkins that runs the entire pipeline from end to end. So, while teams get upskilled on methodology, they also need to upskill on tools that are required to build an infrastructure pipeline.

The tools in Table 8-5 are commonly used across the product lifecycle. The product being referred here is the collection of infrastructure as code scripts for a particular domain. Many organizations have a well-defined archetype toolkit that is standardized in the organization. Of course, there will be reference tools as well for legacy infrastructure. Deciding on the right tools at the beginning is a crucial step toward successful implementation. Some of the tools may be new to the team, and hence they should be upskilled on the new tools and technologies so that during sprint execution, they do not face issues. As more and more stories are delivered, the team steps forward to integrate their pipeline with the service catalog.

Table 8-5. *Pipeline Phases and Commonly Used Tools*

Area	Commonly Used Tools
Planning	JIRA/Snow
Version Control	Git/GitHub
Development	IDEs/SDKs
Build	Ant/Maven
Artifactory	Jfrog
Test	SonarQube/Selenium/Wireshark
Orchestration	Jenkins
Infra Build	Terraform, DRYiCE MyCloud
Deploy	Terraform/Ansible, HCL Launch
Monitor	Solarwinds/Nagios/Zabbix
Security	HCL AppScan
Dashboarding	Grafana/APIs
Documentation	SharePoint/Confluence

Infrastructure as Code Example

Let's look at a scenario where an engineer needs to commission a new VM. They access the ITSM tool like ServiceNow and look for the catalog items that allow them to submit a requisition for provisioning a VM. As soon as the request is approved, the related infrastructure pipeline is autotriggered and sets up the VM without needing any manual intervention. Earlier such requests took two to three weeks of time, but now they just take an hour. Many organizations have realized such benefits and aim to first standardize and automate the basic infrastructure needs that do not need manual inputs. The workflow in Figure 8-4 shows how users are empowered to commission and decommission VMs through the ITSM tool. Once their requests are approved by the approvers, the request is directed to orchestration tools like Jenkins that trigger the respective job. The job further calls out the scripts from the repository for execution. The status after completion is updated in the ITSM tool, thus notifying the user who submitted the ticket. The support team is notified of any issue in the workflow immediately. Similar use cases are identified and implemented in ITSM to facilitate a culture of self-service.

Figure 8-9. *Self-servicing with IaC*

There are multiple tools like Jenkins, TravisCI, etc., available that enable such orchestration and serve as an integration bridge between ITSM and other tools. These tools trigger automation by calling respective jobs that complete an action. This action can be performed by one or more tools. For example, say we have a use case to build an Amazon Machine Image (AMI). This is possible by first spinning up a new virtual machine on AWS, installing the required software, and then building a half-baked AMI, which then becomes a reusable template.

We will design the pipeline that leverages the cloud-native tools to automate a series of jobs as described in Table 8-6.

Table 8-6. *Pipeline Creation Using Cloud-Native Tools*

Tool Name	Purpose
AWS CodeCommit	Another AWS service that hosts secure Git-based repositories.
Jenkins	An open source tool that is used to design and implement pipelines (building CI and CD).
AWS Cloud Formation	An AWS service that helps to design templates that are easy to manage and are repeatable. It helps implement infrastructure as code.

Figure 8-10 describes the integration points between these interfaces. The IaC scripts are versioned in AWS CodeCommit, and Jenkins is configured to trigger the orchestration whenever new changes are updated in AWS CodeCommit.

Figure 8-10. *IaC example on AWS*

Here are the details for this simple IaC pipeline:

1. Jenkins will check out scripts from CodeCommit for any new changes that are seen in the repository. A repository is a container that holds source code that can contain scripts, configuration artifacts, etc., and also IAM permissions to control access to Git repositories.

2. Jenkins is configured to trigger a pipeline on a new change in the Git repository. Similar to the way it calls scripts, Jenkins can easily be configured to call other tools.

3. AWS CFN scripts execute and provision AWS instances using hardened AMI. In the place of CFN scripts, there could be other scripts like Ansible playbooks or Terraform scripts or DRYiCE MyCloud templates that will spin up instances.

4. Once the instance is commissioned, the scripts will further install the software that has been requested, like software, configuration files, or platforms and databases, as needed.

5. The scripts will finally generate an AMI (which is configured), and then the instance is decommissioned, which was provisioned for the creation of the AMI.

Similar use cases are designed that get associated with multiple infrastructure as code pipelines. Each pipeline helps teams to speed up the delivery time and bring down the wait time for application development and testing teams. As pipelines get implemented, the next step for the teams is to integrate the infrastructure pipeline with the application pipeline. The idea is to foster the culture of DevOps wherein both teams understand the product and the underlying infrastructure needs. The IaC repository is also made accessible to development teams to implement more use cases on infrastructure. With this approach the development teams can use APIs provided by the infrastructure as code tools and call those APIs as part of their development pipeline to spin up the infrastructure on demand.

Integrating IaC with Development Pipelines

As IaC matures in the organization, the next step is to integrate and extend the IaC pipelines with other teams. An excellent example for integrating app and infrastructure pipelines is the need for blue-green deployments (see Figure 8-11). This is a best practice that implements the principle of CD, which is possible when the entire end-to-end lifecycle is automated through the pipelines. A blue-green deployment is implemented for every new deployment that has to happen in a production-like environment. So, a new environment is set up, and the new application version is deployed on it. Once it is validated, the existing infrastructure is removed, and the traffic is routed to this new infrastructure.

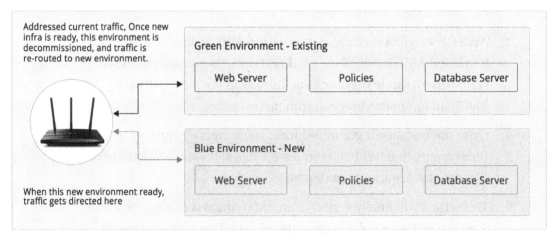

Figure 8-11. *Blue-green deployments*

As new environments replace older environments, this helps to avoid any configuration issues or compatibility issues that normally arise when deploying artifacts on the same environment. All this is made possible with the help of automated tools that are integrated in the pipeline. As a developer checks in code, the CI pipeline verifies the integrity of the code and performs unit tests. All this work is being managed on the developer branch that is detailed either from a feature branch or from the master branch.

Once the code is integrated and tested, it is moved to the development environment where further tests are executed, and the code quality is checked. On success of CI, we move to CD that further enables the movement of binaries from one environment to another. While moving binaries to an environment that must be built on-demand, the IaC pipeline is called. Once the IaC pipeline spins up the required infrastructure, it then deploys the application code on this new infrastructure and notifies stakeholders. Unsuccessful deployments are rolled back, and respective teams are notified to make appropriate changes to rerun the pipeline. See Figure 8-12.

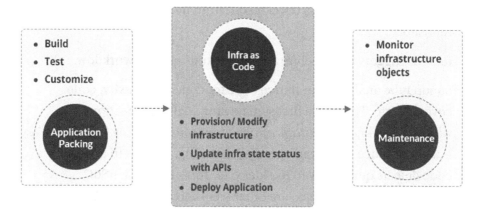

Figure 8-12. *Connecting app and infrastructure workflows*

On the other hand, successful deployments enable monitoring agents that continuously monitor the applications and infrastructure. This cycle is repeated "n" number of times, and every time it is executed, teams get to learn the gaps and improvise.

Extending the IaC Example

Once the IaC pipelines are ready, they can be extended to other teams like the development teams. First, let's look at a basic application pipeline that integrates and tests any new piece of code that gets checked into the source code repository. Later we will deep dive into how to extend an IaC pipeline with application pipeline that leverages the following set of tools:

- *AWS CodeCommit*: Source code versioning

- *Jenkins*: Orchestrating the pipeline

- *ASOC/SonarQube*: Static code analysis

- *JUnit/NUnit*: Unit testing for Java and .NET source code

- *Maven*: Building application source code

- *JFrog Artifactory*: Binary repository

The application pipeline aims to continuously integrate new code thereby practicing the principle of continuous integration. Stories are created and estimated for each step as stated here:

1. The latest source code is checked out from the AWS CodeCommit repository.

2. Jenkins triggers the pipeline and orchestrates the CI workflow.

3. SonarQube analyzes the source code for code complexity, code coverage, etc. This is the first step toward quality inspection, which is also known as *static application security testing* (SAST). It is a key practice encouraging shift-left testing. It helps to analyze code defects quite early in the lifecycle. Tools like HCL ASoC, Fortify, Parasoft JTest, etc., are other well-known tools used in this space.

4. Junit and Nunit test frameworks run unit test cases on the checked-out code to scan for coverage and functionality checks. This is another step toward proactive testing.

5. Apache Maven builds the source code that generates binaries. These binaries are pushed to tools like JFrog Artifactory, which are then pulled when the CD pipeline gets triggered. See Figure 8-13.

Figure 8-13. *AWS CI pipeline example*

The outcome of the previous application pipeline is the artifacts that comprise the latest binaries. These binaries are then deployed to test environments for running functional and performance tests. Gone are those days when test environments had to be blocked for testing. Nowadays, these environments are provisioned on demand using IaC pipelines. The IaC pipeline provisions and configures the new infrastructure, fetches the latest binaries from JFrog Artifactory, and deploys the code. This environment now calls for functional/performance test scripts through tools such as Selenium, Fortify, etc. As pipelines get created and integrated, they can also get integrated with ITSM tools for catalog-based service requests.

Figure 8-14. *Integrating infrastructure and app pipelines*

Figure 8-13 describes how Jenkins triggers the application pipeline first and deploys the binaries. This completes the CI aspect. Once the binaries are ready for deployment, the infrastructure components are provisioned and configured. In this example, it is the AWS AMI that is provisioned. Once the environment is ready, the artifacts are deployed, and this initiates the CD aspect. On this new test instance, the application is tested for regression and functional testing using tools like Selenium. Once the testing is done, the results are published. After this step, the provisioned environment for testing can be decommissioned. This simple scenario had different steps, and each one is managed through a script that is triggered through Jenkins. Implementing such a scenario needs a well-defined plan that identifies the key use cases that should be automated and added in the pipeline. As discussed earlier, these pipelines can be triggered through ITSM tools as well.

Key Agile Practices While Adopting IaC Using Scrum

Here are the key practices:

- Define high-level epics. The previous example can be stated as an epic. This is a large requirement that will have multiple stories.

- Create stories that are linked to the epics and that have an assignee who will work on the stories as per the defined timelines.

- Issues or risks while building the pipeline should be called out in the daily meetings with the team.

- While planning for the sprint, define clear expectations and deliverables with the team.

- Do not aim to deliver a complete pipeline in one sprint; instead, define it across sprints and deliver it continuously as an MVP.

- Each story needs to have a well-defined description and acceptance criteria.

- The team's capacity should be made visible before the sprint starts.

- Encourage team members to lead daily calls and get accountable on their stories.

- Stories can have tasks and avoid subtasks since these become difficult to manage over a period.

- Practice story estimation in every sprint planning meeting.

Summary

The infrastructure as code way of managing infrastructure is replacing the traditional processes in which infrastructure was provisioned, decommissioned, patched, and upgraded. Once the infrastructure teams are trained on the agile concepts and tools, they can start creating a backlog of stories that are prioritized and executed. There are dozens of tools available that the teams can adopt to implement infrastructure as code such as Terraform, Azure Resource Manager (ARM), Puppet, Chef, HCL MyCloud, and other cloud-native tools. The new model brings engineering aspects to infrastructure operations and leverages agile ways of development. The IaC pipeline functions in the same way as the development pipeline where it integrates with multiple tools such as versioning, static code analysis, security analysis, unit testing, build and deployment, testing, etc. To rapidly adopt infrastructure as code and move to agile development, organizations need to focus on the following key areas:

- A clear roadmap with a vision toward IaC adoption

- Identification of tools for source control, testing, deployment, extensions, etc.

- Upscaling teams on understanding the concepts and tools for IaC

- Identification of use cases to be implemented and integrated

- Timelines on when and how the enterprise will offer self-servicing

CHAPTER 9

Success Path

This chapter presents a case study on AgileOps. The topics that will be covered in this chapter are as follows:

- Case study implementing AgileOps

- New operating model for our enterprise Alpha

- Outcomes

In the previous chapter, we looked at the different agile methodologies, frameworks, and implementation approaches to plan and execute the agile journey in the infrastructure operations area. There is no one perfect method that is applicable for all organizations. The decision of which method to choose is tricky and sometimes confusing too. Every framework is supported by agile principles, and there are no strict mandates that must be followed. IT organizations that are keen to transition to agile ways of working know their organization well and thus can decide on which method/framework will benefit them the most. There have been many organizations across multiple industries that have seen success with one method in the initial iterations, while there are other industries that could not succeed with the "as-is" methods but still achieved success by customizing the methods to suit their needs. While application teams adopt agile culture, transitioning the infrastructure operations team is a challenge. Big enterprises plan their transformation roadmap for two to three years with people and automation as their key foundational pillars. While teams get trained on new skills and ceremonies, they also identify new opportunities for automation, and new teams and roles are formed.

© Navin Sabharwal, Raminder Rathore, and Udita Agrawal 2022
N. Sabharwal et al., *Hands-On Guide to AgileOps*, https://doi.org/10.1007/978-1-4842-7505-4_9

Case Study Implementing AgileOps

We have done a deep dive into the processes and best practices and saw practical step-by-step examples of how these are to be used in an infrastructure as code scenario. We will now go through a detailed case study of how the team structures can be created based on what we have learned so far. Our imaginary company Alpha is globally distributed, and the executive board has decided to sponsor the transformation of their infrastructure operations team. The current infrastructure operations team has multiple teams that manage on-premises hardware, network, monitoring, storage, and backup and recently has started supporting cloud operations on AWS and Azure. See Figure 9-1.

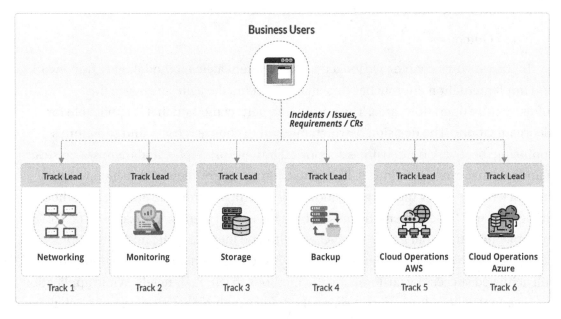

Figure 9-1. *Traditional model for infra IT Ops*

Alpha has also decided that it will not go "big bang" and will initiate the movement to agile with the monitoring team first. The current monitoring team manages and supports multiple tools to monitor thousands of servers and applications. There are predefined thresholds embedded in these tools that actively alert the infrastructure engineer through emails. This engineer manually checks the alert, resolves the underlying issue, and updates the knowledge database (KEDB). The key expectation of transitioning this team first is to modernize the way alerts are addressed. Also, applications are moving to cloud. Alpha creates a roadmap with a clear vision to adopt

AI-driven operations in two years. Funds are being planned and approved for this new organization change as well as for investing in new tools and upskilling teams on new technologies.

A centralized and dedicated team called AIOps is formed for implementing, tracking, and executing this new transformation roadmap. The members of this team are consultants and practitioners who write out the details and define the new structure to be rolled out. They assess the current monitoring team on the following key factors:

- Agile competency on Scrum/Kanban

- Expertise on new technology

- Current operations workload

- Current project workload

- Team performance with metrics like cycle time

- Automation scenarios implemented in the past

While the prerequisites are assessed and baselined, the team decides to restructure the team as shown in Table 9-1.

Table 9-1. *Comparison of Traditiona IT Ops and Agile IT Ops*

Team Name	Agile Method	Remarks
BAU-Generic ops	Kanban	Transition traditional operational support for monitoring to agile ways. Team members "pull" work and get more accountable.
CTB-Infrastructure ops	Scrum	A new team is created from the BAU that creates IaC pipelines for the prioritized use cases on automation.
AIOps team	Scrum	Another new team is formed, through a combination of reskilling and hiring, that works on AIOps. This team runs the sprints for deploying AIOps in the environment.

The team will also create a workflow that defines how monitoring alerts will respond post-transformation. Every monitoring alert will be tracked through the ITSM tool. These alerts will be created by AIOps or by end users or business users. A clear vision for AIOps is also set up that will transform the way alerts will be responded in the new ecosystem.

AIOps will be helpful only when it is able to autoresolve the monitoring issues when integrated with intelligent runbook automation tools. The management at Alpha has evaluated tools with event correlation capabilities and has funded its implementation that will be rolled out in phases.

Note that there are numerous tools available like Moogsoft, Splunk, Zenoss, and automated remediation tools like DRYiCE iAutomate that are enabling organizations to speed up the incident resolution processes and also serve as the right tools for the SREs. See Figure 9-2.

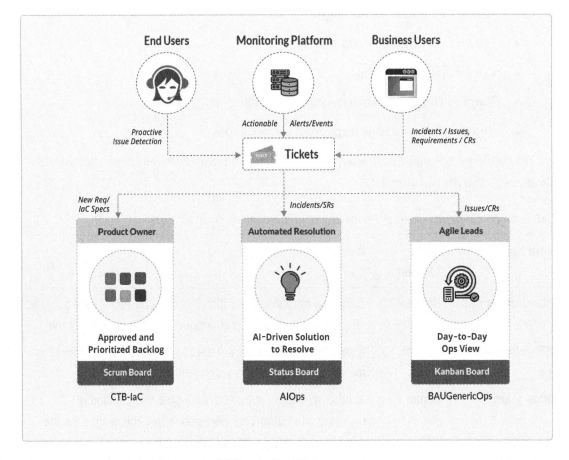

Figure 9-2. *New working model for Infra IT Ops*

New Operating Model for Alpha

Here is the new operating model:

- *CTB-IaC team*: This is the automation team. New requirements related to infra setups will be managed through IaC pipelines. This team will work in Scrum mode and will deliver pipelines based on the requirements that are prioritized and approved. This team will build reusable templates that are version controlled and orchestrated through the ITSM tool. They will also pay attention to various important infrastructure components such as network, firewall, RBAC implementation, etc., while building the pipelines.

- *AIOps team*: This is a team that will configure the new solution to monitor and autoresolve commonly faced issues. They will identify the use cases and feed data into the solution. The AIOps systems will leverage analytics and machine learning features to make the right decision; for example, it will autoresolve the issue and update the ITSM tool. All identified use cases will be discussed and configured in the system with help from the BAU-GenericOps team. Every use case that will be managed by the AIOps solution will be targeted to reduce ticket volume and ensure an increase in system availability. This team will start the project in Scrum mode to deliver the core features and functionality and then move to Kanban when the project moves to the operations phase, while still continuing to run sprints for enhancements and updates.

- *BAU-GenericOps*: This is the traditional infra operations team that will get transitioned into an agile operations team by practicing Kanban to resolve interruptions and other day-to-day operation activities. Alerts or tickets that are not being resolved by the AIOps solution will be pulled for quick resolution by this team. This team will continue to track the issues and resolutions and also update their knowledge database (KEDB). They will also collaborate with the other two teams to automate use cases in the AIOps solution as much as possible.

Outcomes

The end goal is to optimize and automate whatever is possible in the monitoring space. The inception will have the three teams, but moving forward as AIOps becomes matured, the other BAU-GenericOps team should become lean. Alpha will accrue multiple benefits by implementing such a model.

- *Collaboration*: Highly connected engineering teams that are cross-skilled and work closely with product teams with one common vision to deliver and support a quality system to end customers.

- *Resiliency*: The ability to design, build, and deploy systems that are well tested and compliant.

- *Self-service*: Empowered product teams to scale systems as needed in their delivery pipeline.

- *Shift-left security*: The ability to embed security policies in the system at every stage.

- *Continuous improvement*: The ability to learn and scale with every iteration. Automate as much as possible with AIOps to provide the required tools and technologies to agile and SRE teams to realize their goals of reducing toil quickly and increasing availability.

Summary

Every organization has unique requirements, ways of working, current structures, and business goals. Various ways in which infrastructure teams can be organized using agile infrastructure operations were covered in this chapter. This can serve as guidance while designing the organization structures and processes. The transformation needs to be phased and planned based on the organizational needs and constraints. Teams should be ready to test and fail and then improve. Every model emphasizes agile and DevOps practices such as CI/CD, infrastructure as code, site reliability engineering, Scrum, Kanban, etc. At the end of the day, what matters is that the transformation should create and nourish a culture of trust and visibility. New tools and technologies do empower teams, but if they are not used effectively, then the vision to be agile will fade.

CHAPTER 10

Learnings and Ways Forward

In this chapter, we will be discussing what the next steps are for an enterprise. The topics that will be covered in this chapter are as follows:

- Our learnings

- Emerging trends to focus on

- Next steps

- Conclusion

With the growth in areas like the cloud, microservices-based architecture, site reliability engineering, and so on, organizations are rethinking how they should operate. They have learned that agility with resiliency and automation is the need of the hour. While many have already started their transition to this new norm, there are teams that need to switch to the new working style quickly before it is too late. So, this chapter covers what we have learned and how to move forward.

Our Learnings

Here is what we have learned:

- Set up a small team to automate infrastructure; this is the team that adopts infrastructure as code principles and tools. This team can reside with the infra hierarchy or sit between the apps and ops teams. Some organizations call these teams the DevOps team.

© Navin Sabharwal, Raminder Rathore, and Udita Agrawal 2022
N. Sabharwal et al., *Hands-On Guide to AgileOps*, https://doi.org/10.1007/978-1-4842-7505-4_10

- Create a central repository of reusable artifacts and templates that can be used by developers as well. This way you are empowering application teams to set up environments on their own. If you want to speed operations up, invest in cloud lifecycle management and AIOps tools like Moogsoft, Zenoss, DRYiCE iAutomate, and DRYiCE MyCloud.

- Identify and prioritize use cases that can be automated, such as looking at ways to integrate the infra pipeline with the application pipelines.

- Baseline where you are today and track the improvements regularly. This becomes a good case for other teams to refer to and adopt.

- If you are on the digital path, then plan for adopting AIOps. Automation is a key lever to driver agility.

- Embed security principles across the pipeline to avoid vulnerabilities and ensure that work is delivered as per the defined compliance rules.

- If the need arises, revisit the team structure and define new roles to boost team morale. Also introduce trainings to team members on new technologies.

Emerging Trends to Focus

Technology can speed up the deployment of capabilities, but ultimately it is people who need to use these technologies to their potential and realize the benefits. Thus, people and cultural change are the keys to attaining maturity in agile infrastructure operations. New roles are being introduced to encourage teams to adopt this new cultural change wherein teams work toward a common vision, leverage common tools and platforms, and are upskilled to new technologies like the cloud, infrastructure as code, AIOps, and of course methodologies like agile. Standardizing infrastructure setups, rationalizing tools, identifying opportunities to automate, and removing waste are all key drivers toward running an AgileOps team. With all these new trends, if teams are not ready for the changes, roadmaps will slow down. Hence, it's important that teams are upskilled on new technologies and processes and investments are thought through.

Figure 10-1. *Some key IT trends*

Just implementing an agile tool will not suffice. Understanding the needs and practicing the concepts are important. Additionally, the success lies in team collaboration and continuously improving as teams scale up on their path toward agility. The transition from traditional to agile gets successful with the guidance of an agile coach or a practitioner who creates a roadmap with milestones, guides the teams to move away from time-consuming processes, adopts new modern platforms, measures and tracks metrics, and mentors teams on the new methods and practices. The coach partners with teams to define the new strategy that is rolled in phases and continuously monitors the progress for realigning the plan as need be. However, since applying agile to infrastructure operations is niche and emerging, this book aims to provide guidance from real-world implementations that can be leveraged for fast-tracking the journey toward agile infrastructure operations. New guidance and data will be constantly made available and updated at the companion site http://agileinfraops.com so that the readers can further enhance their knowledge on this subject on a continuous basis. We would love to hear from our readers with their comments, feedback, and success stories of deploying agile for cloud, infrastructure, and application operations at feedback@ agileinfraops.com.

Organizations are also looking at how they can bring agility to their legacy infrastructure that carries legacy applications. New customer demands have paved the way to revisit how applications are developed and interact with other components or applications. Some organizations have plans to modernize legacy applications and move them to the cloud using cloud-native and container technologies. Containerization has helped many organizations to deploy applications anytime and anywhere without facing issues around configuration, connectivity, compatibility, etc. Supporting this technology demands smart tools that empower application teams to build and deploy applications. Tools like Docker, Kubernetes, etc., are being piloted and adopted by teams for better management of resources and applications.

Teams can accrue maximum benefits by implementing the right technology and practicing agile in iterations. The current era is all about unlearning and learning new skills and continuously evolving. Teams can move toward this goal only if they are equipped with the right ecosystem that focuses on removing barriers between teams. Whether it is Scrum or Kanban, until teams understand the importance of the methodology, they will not be able to progress. If an organization is getting started with IaC, then Scrum is an ideal fit. On the other hand, if traditional ops is to be transformed, then Kanban is an ideal fit. This decision can easily be made with the help of a coach who can assess the team structure and current working model and make relevant recommendations. Such recommendations are prioritized and mapped with milestones that have defined timelines.

We also accept the fact that the infra ops cannot work in silos with their rigid processes anymore. They have to collaborate with dev teams, QA teams, and security teams to ensure that product deliveries are well integrated and that they can quickly reach out to the end customers. And this is achieved by finding use cases that bridge the gap between these teams. Educating the teams on using modern platforms that provide flexibility and end-to-end visibility makes sure that in the long run these teams become cohesive in nature. Modern technologies like the cloud, serverless computing, edge computing, software-defined infrastructure, and AIOps are all encouraging organizations to switch to agile working models that will deliver faster results. So, the need for moving the infrastructure toward modernization and digitalization is because the applications are also getting upgraded or modernized. Both the development and operational worlds need to connect and collaborate to deliver efficient results. This is possible when they stop resisting changes and deploy these changes faster. An agile mindset acts as a booster in this direction. Mentoring the teams on the benefits of agile and helping them to become agile is essential for continued growth. And yes, incentives and funding are crucial to ignite this journey. A well-planned enterprise strategy is needed that addresses security, compliance, regulations, risks, and resiliency with the base foundation set on agility.

Next Steps

Agile has been evolving since 2001, and today it has become a must for every IT organization that needs to survive. Some call it a project management approach, and others call it a way of working. The rest are associating this as just a "process change that leads toward lean." In any case, the term *agile organizations* is trending, and it means an organization where applications, operations, and other connected teams work in an agile mode. These institutions design, develop, and operate products five times faster. Various agile methods have also been modified, and hybrid versions applicable to different scenarios are available for use. Collaborating, staying relevant, swiftly overcoming unexpected changes, and moving from "doing agile" to "being agile" are all on an evolving journey that organizations cannot ignore. As this journey moves ahead, value-based decisions will be important. Companies need to deliver value to their customers instead of just focusing on quantity. They need to stay close to their customers to get their feedback and improvise continuously.

Talking about an infrastructure operations team, the value that they can deliver is the way they operate and set up environments, the mode of communication, and above all "doing agile." This will be achieved through optimized processes that deliver what is needed. There must be trust and transparency between teams and a single pane of truth for everyone, a standard set of tools and automation to leverage, and a well-defined framework to reuse and improvise. Self-managed teams will emerge that will continue to drive success factors. As companies reinvent themselves, teams will become more manageable. In fact, some call it a *flat structure* when power and accountability are distributed.

Collaboration with Security will no longer be in silos; and methods and tools will be introduced that automate security checks at every stage of the development and operations pipelines. For example, IaC teams will continue to introduce security checks in their pipeline to check on various aspects such as compliance scores, vulnerability issues, policy compliance, etc., and proceed only if successful. Technical debt will be monitored to capture the improvement. Repetitive actions will continue to be automated, thus leading to lean and AI-led operations.

Conclusion

If you have not started on your agile journey, then it is not too late. You should identify your needs, select the right agile framework, and evolve. Combining the best of agile, DevOps, SRE, lean, and DevOps will help you to foster collaboration, improve productivity, and mature toward "being agile."

Above all, you need a plan with a clear vision that progresses you toward success. The need for agile is no longer optional; it is the new way to operate, and it is high time that your teams adopt this approach and build an ecosystem for self-managed teams that are accountable, cross-skilled, and ready for new challenges!

Index

© Navin Sabharwal, Raminder Rathore, and Udita Agrawal 2022
N. Sabharwal et al., *Hands-On Guide to AgileOps*, https://doi.org/10.1007/978-1-4842-7505-4

K

T

U, V

W, X, Y, Z

Printed in the United States
by Baker & Taylor Publisher Services